PHILOSOPHICAL
ANTHROPOLOGY

PHILOSOPHICAL ANTHROPOLOGY

by MICHAEL LANDMANN

Translated by David J. Parent

THE WESTMINSTER PRESS
PHILADELPHIA

Translated from the German *Philosophische Anthropologie,* © 1969 Walter de Gruyter & Co., Berlin

PUBLISHED BY THE WESTMINSTER PRESS®

PHILADELPHIA, PENNSYLVANIA

PRINTED IN THE UNITED STATES OF AMERICA

Library of Congress Cataloging in Publication Data

Landmann, Michael, 1913–
   Philosophical anthropology.

   Bibliography: p.
   1. Philosophical anthropology. I. Title.
BD450.L24813   128   73–20484
ISBN 0–664–20995–5

CONTENTS

FOREWORD
TO THE
AMERICAN EDITION

Philosophical anthropology is not always included in the ranks of classical philosophical disciplines: metaphysics, epistemology, logic, ethics. Yet, in its substantive origins, it also dates back to Greek philosophy. In the Renaissance and the Age of Goethe it reached new peaks. And in our century it was reestablished in the 1920's by Helmuth Plessner and Max Scheler and continued by Adolf Portmann, Erich Rothacker, and Arnold Gehlen. Descartes and Kant had made "awareness" the "constitutive basis" of philosophical reality; like Humboldt's linguistics, philosophical anthropology is one of the many attempts to formulate this basis more concretely and more comprehensively. From this point of view, it is not merely the study of "one segment of the world among others" but it claims to be a new, ultimate foundation, a "transcendental philosophy."

But its revival in the '20s did not stem from internal philosophical motives. It became actual, at that time, as a countercurrent to nineteenth-century positivism with its tendency to fragmentate the world, because of an awakening need for the introduction of a "view of the whole." This need, which is a philosophical one that, after a century of natural science, general philosophy can no longer satisfy, made itself felt simultaneously in numerous sciences. One way to satisfy this need was the synthetic reconstruction of these sciences from an anthropological perspective. In addition, the human and social sciences, which for decades had been following the pattern set by the natural sciences, now were beginning to reflect upon their own methods and goals. Anthropology was the trend of the times. In part under the influence of philosophical anthropology, in part independently, there arose in German-speaking countries the disciplines of psychological, pedagogical, political, theological, and medical anthropology, which still continue to this day.

For readers of French or English, access to philosophical anthropology and to these various subdisciplines is impeded by an external linguistic difficulty: in these languages the word "anthropology" is already occupied by natural-scientific somatic anthropology and by the prevalence of the ethnological approach. In this book the word "anthropology" is used in a broader and more fundamental meaning. In content, however, the reader will rediscover, under a changed perspective, many things which in his country are familiar topics of specialized disciplines. Educational psychology's concept of "self-conditioning" recurs in the more broadly formulated anthropological expression "the self-domestication of man." The psychology of creativity has philosophical antecedents in the doctrine of free human self-formation and work (Pico della Mirandola, the Storm and Stress movement). Points of contact exist between philosophical anthropology and animal psychology because an important procedure in anthropology is the comparison of man with the animals (environment and instinct in the animals, "openness to the world" and self-shaped behavior in man). The concept of the "whole," familiar in America from *Gestalt* theory, contributed, as was mentioned above, to the origin of philosophical anthropology. "Complexity reduction" is a main tendency in Gehlen's anthropology, according to which man, not like other animals equipped with perception "filters," is exposed to a flood of stimuli that he must organize by language and by the selection of particular institutions. Insofar as philosophical anthropology today no longer defines man only in terms of his power of abstraction or his ability to distinguish between good and evil, but, like behaviorism, places him firmly in his natural environment, in his cultural world, and studies him as a being determined by history, culture, and tradition, it converges but does not coincide completely with fundamental works of American cultural anthropology (for instance, by Kroeber).

From its inception, philosophical anthropology has met with opposition. Metaphysics considers it not sufficiently general and fundamental; individual sciences consider it too much so. Existentialism was its competitor in the '20s. Karl Jaspers has reproached it with reifying and fixating man by speaking of him in the third person instead of the first, which always remains an open possibility. The Marxist camp today repeats the same argument from a different point of view: like ontology, philosophical anthropology establishes permanent structures and thus fails to recognize the essentially historical and changing nature of man. According to this view, philosophical anthropology is a form of naturalism resulting from the loss of a future-oriented philosophy of history (as also Odo Marquard). Another Marxist objection is the accusation that anthropology starts with the individual rather than with society or the "complex of conditions." Marxists consider anthropology too unhistorical. On the other hand, structuralists see it as too historical, as overestimating the individual when in reality the motive forces are located in subconscious universal constants.

Despite these easily exposable misunderstandings, philosophical anthropology has survived both as a school of philosophy and as a methodological viewpoint outside of philosophy. It is even having repercussions in Eastern bloc countries where men who seek to transform historical materialism have linked it with the young Marx's "Paris manuscripts" (Adam Schaff in Poland, the Yugoslavian *Praxis* group). In Germany it has recently proven its fecundity by generating a new branch called "anthropology of knowledge" (K. O. Apel). Thus, this author hopes that the American public too will draw some benefit from the observations and ideas that are presented in this general introduction to philosophical anthropology.

I thank the translator, my colleague David J. Parent, with whom it was always a pleasure to work. I thank the publisher, The Westminster Press, for undertaking the risk of publishing a book from an unfamiliar philosophical and cultural field.

MICHAEL LANDMANN

The Free University of Berlin

TRANSLATOR'S NOTE

The German original of Landmann's PHILOSOPHICAL ANTHRO-
POLOGY has become a standard authority in its field. There are
translations into Spanish and Japanese, and the more recently
published Dutch translation is enjoying great success. The
need for an American translation is compelling both for the intrinsic value of the book and also because, apart from Max
Scheler's *Man's Place in Nature* and Adolf Portmann's *New
Paths in Biology*, very few books on philosophical anthropology, an ascendant trend in contemporary German thought,
have appeared in English. Such important anthropologists as
Helmuth Plessner, Erich Rothacker and Arnold Gehlen are
scarcely known to readers of English. This book reports about
all of them, and it elucidates the connection between anthropology as a philosophical discipline and the anthropological point of view that pervades all the moral and social sciences. It also deals with the relations between German
philosophical anthropology and American cultural anthropology and with the difference between philosophical anthropology and the "image of man" implicit in all religion and
art.

Like the original, this translation is written, for the most
part, in nontechnical language. It is based mainly on the
second edition, except for two major sections, on existentialism
and on Marxism, which are additions from the third.

The translator greatly admires the clarity, brilliance, and broad synthetic power of Professor Landmann's original work, and it is not false modesty to hope that these qualities will, to some degree, shine through in the translation.

DAVID J. PARENT

Illinois State University

Part 1

INTRODUCTION TO PHILOSOPHICAL ANTHROPOLOGY

CHAPTER 1

The Meaning of
Philosophical Anthropology

Scientific, Ethnological, and
Philosophical Anthropology

PHILOSOPHICAL ANTHROPOLOGY is the title of this book. This already implies that other types of anthropology exist.

First of all, the natural sciences have a somatophysical anthropology as a branch of biology. This biological anthropology was established as early as the second half of the eighteenth century (by Daubenton, Blumenbach, Sömmering). However, the term "anthropology" goes back to the age of humanism: the Protestant humanist O. Casmann in 1596 published a book by that title. The nineteenth century then witnessed the establishment of anthropological societies all over the world. At first, scientific anthropology was mainly the science of the various races of man, and its primary method of determining racial differences was skull measurement. When, however, in the middle of the nineteenth century, skeletons of men from older geological epochs were also found—first the famous Neanderthal man, prematurely labeled *homo primigenius*—anthropology, on the basis of these diluvial findings of human remains, undertook the additional task of reconstructing the natural history of mankind, the *Hominidae*. Meanwhile the idea had been proposed that the relationship between man and the apes, the anthropoids, a fact that had always been known, could be interpreted in the sense of the genesis of the human race from the animal kingdom. Thus the study of the origin of man was also added to the objectives of scientific anthropology. More recently the study of human heredity has been classified by some as a part of anthropology.

But only in the nineteenth century, when science totally dominated the scene, could this physiological anthropology usurp exclusive claim to the name "anthropology." Casmann, the humanist, had a much broader concept of anthropology: to him it was the *doctrina geminae naturae humanae*, the study of the psychophysical dual nature of man, and this broader application of the term was accepted as valid until well into the eighteenth century. In Germany today, now that the predominantly scientific age is over, Casmann's definition is again gaining currency.

In contrast, in England and France, and to some extent in America, anthropology is equated with ethnology, of which prehistory is also considered a part. This discipline, like the anthropological study of races, also investigates differences among men—not mainly in the physical, however, but in cultural aspects. Even in Germany this use of the term is not completely unknown. Wilhelm Mühlmann's *Geschichte der Anthropologie* (1948) is mainly, if not exclusively, a history of ethnology.

How, then, does the field of philosophical anthropology differ? This much can be said in advance: physical and ethnological anthropology both presuppose knowledge about the nature of man and examine merely his external characteristics or cultural achievements. Philosophy, on the other hand, investigates precisely the knowledge that these sciences take for granted and inquires into the fundamental ontological structures that constitute man in contrast to all other beings that exist.

However, even this most general delineation of the objectives of philosophical anthropology meets with difficulties. An extreme advocate of natural science could object: Does man really represent a separate section of reality calling for a special discipline to study him? Perhaps he is only an animal like the others, differing from them no more than other beings differ from one another; just as we do not have a philosophy of birds and fish, possibly anthropology too is unnecessary. Included in the philosophy of organic life, it might require at most a chapter in animal psychology.

A second problem that arises right at the start is the following: Exactly what is the objective of our research when we inquire into the nature of man? Are we looking for properties that must be manifested in all men who have ever lived or will ever live, in all cultures, or, in other words, for a criterion enabling us to determine whether or not a being is a man at all? Or is that perhaps only a preliminary question and are we really concerned rather with developing the highest potentials of mankind, which not every man or even every culture attains but which manifest truly and perfectly what it really means to be a man? In other words, are we looking for the nadir, the lowest point of his being, where the term "man" can first be correctly applied, or for the apex, the highest point of his being, the ideal of man—if there is such a thing—which he often falls short of?

The Influence of Human Self-interpretation on Human Self-formation

At the very beginning of philosophical anthropology we have to make clear to ourselves one unusual and important fact: man's knowledge of man is not without effect on man's being. Normally, knowledge does not produce any change in the thing known. Things have a firm structure and constitution of their own, and knowledge coming from the outside does not encroach upon them. Being, as Nicolai Hartmann formulated it, is "overwhelmingly indifferent" toward being known. Man, on the contrary—and only he—is an exception to this general rule. Or, more cautiously stated, only his most general structure, the special modality of his perception and actions, etc., is given him by nature as a firm heritage. This element of firmness is, however, not all there is to man. Above this rises a second dimension not determined by nature but left to his own creative power and decision. Even his manner of providing himself with food—whether by gathering, hunting, agriculture, or cattle raising—is not dictated by instinct; he has to adapt his methods of obtaining food to the respective country or climate, and can perfect them through experience and invention. Whether monogamy or polygamy will prevail and which of the many possible types of polygamy, whether the structure of the family will be patriarchal or matriarchal, whether the family itself is to comprise the largest social unit or several families join together in more comprehensive groups, whether a strict hierarchy will dominate communal life or every man have the same rights and duties—for all this and also for the higher areas of religion, art, or science there are no mandatory norms anchored in man's nature. All this is "culture." And by definition culture is created by man's own free initiative, and that is why he gives it such a multiplicity of forms, differing from people to people and from age to age (see Part 5). But in creating culture, man creates himself.

What has been said up to this point of the species "man" also applies, other things being equal, to individual men. The individual too is equipped by nature with certain predispositions of character and intellect; but what he makes of these natural tendencies and what sort of man he wants to be is, to a more or less determinable extent, left to himself. Man has no mandate to "become the person he is." Quite the contrary: there takes place in him what Bergson defined as "creation of oneself by oneself." However, it was only relatively late in history that man became aware that he is his own creator as well as the creator of his culture. In primeval times his consciousness merely imitated mythical prototypes and expanded on traditional patterns. But actually even this was always done with a personal style. For the Greeks and even more for modern man, the individual shaping of one's own personality and life is even a basic postulate. The responsibility merely to repeat a preexistent pattern is no longer the only possibility, and man has come to realize that his greatest and most beautiful task is to construct his life after models of his own choosing or, without any models, according to his own principles.

All this could be summed up in Nietzsche's phrase to the effect that man is "the still undetermined animal." However, this sounds as if man's indeterminacy were only a defect and man could and would someday attain determinacy. And that is not the case. Man is, in contrast with the animals, essentially indeterminate. That is, his life does not follow a preestablished course, but nature has, as it were, let him go only half finished. The other half has been left for him to finish. Man is the being that, according to Plessner and Gehlen, still has work to do on himself, namely, to complete, as it were, his own creation. This is true both of nations and epochs as regards the cultural institutions in which human life is lived, as well as of individuals as regards the ultimate decisions by which each masters his own existence. Man not only lives, but he leads his life (Gehlen).

And precisely this—that he is not univocally determinate and may and must yet shape himself—is the basis of the effect that self-interpretation has on man's being. Self-interpretations become ideals and objectives that regulate self-formation (Theodor Litt). Man is his own creator in two ways: he makes himself, and he also decides what to make himself into (Ortega y Gasset).

However, not all self-formation of man takes place because of a conscious or subconscious image he has of himself. Often he is impelled from the outside rather than self-determined. Even when he thinks he knows the motives of his actions, he is often really acting from quite different impulses. In the Middle Ages, heretics were burned supposedly from care for the good of their souls, but were not greed and sadism also involved? Every realization of an idea contains a further element not yet expressly stipulated in the original idea ("when God created the dawn, he was startled to find it so beautiful"), and as reality it becomes subject to the law of development: in the course of time it necessarily takes on new meanings and it may in fact finally represent the exact opposite of the original concept and fact.

Nonetheless it would be foolish to dispute the intrinsic connection between the great self-images mankind always designs of itself and the concomitant shaping of cultural and personal life. Mankind's self-interpretation, its conception of itself, its essence, and its destiny, is not without influence on what it then in fact is. The Greeks, for example, conceived of man as primarily a rational being; though that is in part already the expression of a culture directed toward rationality, at the same time this anthropology has a reciprocal effect on the culture: it tends to make men want more and more to be what they think they are by nature, and to seek as rational beings to live more and more by reason. The Greek ethic, which pits reason against the desires and requires it to subdue them, is intelligible only in this context and as a result of this image of man. For Christianity, however, man is a being whose ontological center of gravity lies not in this world but in the beyond: this leads to the medieval structure of life, in which secular cultural areas are less strongly developed and not autonomous, but depend rather on the primary cultural institution, the church, since it alone establishes the transcendental connection with the beyond. For the early modern period, in turn, man is the being whose soul responds to the infinity of the world with a similarly infinite desire and striving, and the result is a culture of unbounded expansionism in all areas, colored by enthusiasm for progress and for the future. A corresponding image of man is always at the basis of the formation of every cultural domain, of every artistic style, and every social order (therefore the term "political anthropology" is used today). Every cultural creation contains a secret or cryptic anthropology.

This confirms that man's image of his being does affect his being itself. He always retains his openness and adaptability, but he also has to strive constantly for completion and determinacy. Therefore the concepts with which he seeks to comprehend his own existence do exercise a determining force on the self-realization of his existence. Man's respective idea of himself becomes the ideal that guides and shapes him.

This shows the ultimate significance of anthropology. At the same time it shows that anthropology inevitably accompanies man. Man does not, like other beings, simply exist, but he inquisitively asks about and interprets himself; the concept of man (*anthrōpos*) implies anthropology. This is not mere optional, theoretical speculation; it springs from the deepest necessity of a being that must shape itself and therefore needs an orientational model or *Leitbild* to go by. Man's incompletion is compensated for by self-understanding, which tells him how he can perfect himself. His interpretation of himself does not stand separate from an immutable reality; rather, although intending merely to interpret, it has a formative effect on that reality.

CHAPTER 2

Prephilosophical Anthropology

Self-knowledge is what Pascal regards as the very heart of man's greatness. In his commentary on Psalm 8 he says: man is so weak and small that a drop of water can kill him. Yet he is nobler than what kills him, for he knows that he dies, he knows that the universe is stronger than he. The universe, despite all its grandeur, does not know of its grandeur. Therefore man by his knowledge, even if it be only knowledge of his smallness, remains superior to the universe.

Not only philosophy, however, contains knowledge of man about himself. One of Dilthey's main achievements was that he called attention to the fact that all life is intrinsically hermeneutic. It always has an interpretation of itself at hand. This is not an extrinsic and secondary trait but a very property of life, and this reflectivity that accompanies life seemed to Dilthey even richer and wiser than the abstractions of conceptual thought. As every man, consciously or subconsciously, has a *Weltanschauung*, or world view, he also has, prior to all philosophy, a view of man. Every cultural product, even the earliest religion and art, contains an image of man. It contains it without making any general statement about his nature, purely by the way he is depicted, by what is established as his predominant trait, what is expected of him. But occasionally it also is expressed in universal statements.

One example of how, even at an early intellectual level, the question of man comes up and seeks an answer is given in a myth of the Incas: three times, it is reported, the gods sought to create man. The first time they made him of clay; but the clay man was so stupid and clumsy that the enraged gods immediately destroyed him again and formed a new man out of wood. But this attempt too failed, for the wooden man was so coarse and malicious that he too had to be destroyed. But a few wooden men escaped destruction and fled into the forest; there they comprise the nation of the monkeys. The third time the gods made a man out of dough. The dough-men were clever, but sly. The wearied gods decided, however, to let them live despite their imperfection, but they fogged up their brains so that their cleverness would not save them from errors and they could not discover the ultimate secrets of this world.

For the inventor of the myth, the similarity between man and the apes had obviously already become a problem and he tried to explain it by considering the monkeys imperfect models of man. Moreover, he notes man's cleverness as his outstanding trait, but at the same time he is surprised that man, nonetheless, is fallible and not all-knowing, and so he also gives a mythical explanation for this.

Anthropomorphism and Its Conquest

It seems natural to us men of the Western world, because of our religious and humanistic traditions, that man assumes a unique and special position in the world. Both the Bible and the Greeks attribute a special position to man. Yet the contrasting of man and animal is a thought that first had to be conceived (and did not go unchallenged). Many primitive tribes do not even have a comprehensive concept for animals such as is necessary in order to contrast them with man. Primitive man often never becomes aware of his superiority to the animals; he believes that they too have a language and a village of their own in the jungle, and thus he has no idea that only he has a culture. In fact, he often sees superiority

as being on the side of the animals. In Greek mythology the
centaur Chiron is the teacher of Achilles and other heroes,
instructing them not only in the knowledge of medicinal herbs
but also in zither-playing: "the noble pedagogue who to his
glory educated a race of heroes." In Democritus, man learns
culture from the animals, song from the birds, hunting with
nets from the spider, etc. The Cynics also gave importance to
the example of the animals. Fairy tales also tell of the higher
intelligence and adroitness of the animals. For Romanticism,
animals are closer to the secrets of nature than man, who is
an intellectualized and reflective creature. That animals are
even considered superior beings stems from their simultaneous
similarity and dissimilarity to man, by which they inspire a
numinous awe—and the numinous is always associated with
greater value.

The culture of India regards plants, animals, and men as
beings of the same level and rank that together form "a great
democracy of being" (Groethuysen). Therefore the Indian
mentality accepts the transmigration of souls between men and
animals without difficulty. The basis of this attitude, however,
is not only the elevation of plants and animals to a level com-
parable to man's, but the idea of a single universal foundation
of existence that is the unifying principle behind all particular
things, whose individuation is only illusory appearance. All
individuality emerges for only a moment like a wave out of
the sea of fundamental reality and sinks back into it, possibly
to emerge again elsewhere in another individuality. The existent thing does not, as in the Greek view, have the center of
gravity of its own being in its form, which distinguishes it
from other things, but in universal being. Therefore, Greek and
Indian thought represent diametrically opposite possibilities
of world view. The Greeks love form, therefore they are an
aesthetic people; they love the single object, therefore they are
the founders of science. All this is less pronounced in the
Indians. Greek ethics regards the human person as an ultimate
reality; it puts the individual under his own command. Indian

ethics, on the contrary, promises redemption of the person through final dissolution in the formless basic reality of the world.

Primitive totemism also stems from an original feeling of man's relationship with the animals. Many native tribes believe they are related especially closely with a particular animal. In this totem animal the tribe honors its ancestor and it regards the animal as a constantly effective source of strength. The individual members of the tribe tend to identify with this animal.

One field anthropologist reports a conversation he had with a native whose race regarded the otter as their totem animal. An otter just then happened to be crossing a nearby river. The man said: "Look, how beautifully I am swimming across the river!" To all objections that he only meant that this animal was his protective spirit, that a special stream of energy linked him with it, and the like, the native insisted firmly that he himself was really this otter.

In general the limits of the individual personality were originally broader than they are for us today. In many early cultures weapons and utensils were buried with the dead. Usually this is explained by the assumption that the dead will continue to use these things in the afterlife. Another explanation holds that these implements, which the deceased always had on his person in life, on which he himself carved magic symbols, and which he made use of on hundreds of occasions, are therefore seen as one entity with him; somehow they belong to his total appearance like the limbs of the body, and they still contain something of his power. Perhaps he could still inflict harm on his enemies even though he is dead. And therefore these objects must follow him to the grave. The burning of widows in India may probably also have stemmed from a similar feeling. Often natives who had sold their land to Europeans and withdrawn into the interior returned after a few weeks and months and wanted their lands back, in many cases even without returning the purchase price. They felt so intimately connected with this property that had belonged to them for generations, it was for them such an integral component of their entire being, that they could not understand that a single and merely rational event like a sale could separate it definitively from them. Even in our own cultural world both the self-esteem and the social prestige of men are often measured by their material possessions. On the other hand, the ancient Stoics taught that not only possessions but even the body itself is, compared with our true inner self, an opposite, external thing, and Christianity teaches a similar doctrine. The modern humanist agrees with this to some extent but he cannot desist from also counting the body as part of the self and admiring others for their strength and beauty. So we live alternately in personality circles of varying radius.

One instance of the general phenomenon of anthropomorphism is that early man did not feel opposed or superior to the animals. The humanization of the animal is a particular case of humanization in general. In the strict sense, anthropomorphism means that man sees natural phenomena as embodying higher beings patterned on man and that he endows his gods with his own form. Xenophanes the Eleatic in his day opposed the anthropomorphism of the Homeric Olympus with the argument that the oxen could with equal right picture their gods in the form of oxen.[1] In a broader sense, however, anthropomorphism is every understanding of the world by analogy with man. According to the admittedly disputed theory of animatism, primitive man regarded all nature as having a soul, because he subconsciously projected his own soul into it, as children still do today. When a stone rolls down the mountain, the primitive does not think that this is because of its weight, but because it wants to. Animation, however, does not necessarily imply personification. There is a distinction between the diffuse universal imputation of soul by animatism and the personification characteristic of animism. But botany texts of the nineteenth century also contain anthropomorphic statements, e.g., when they say that the tropical plants had grown "accustomed" to the sun. The authors of such texts started naïvely from the point of view of man, who could not bear so much sun, whereas the completely different organism of a tropical plant is equipped from the start for more sun and does not have to become accustomed to it. Goethe correctly said: "Man never realizes how anthropomorphic he is."

Yet although we can never break completely from anthropomorphism, some of its grosser forms were eliminated early in history not only by philosophy but even in the prephilosophical intellectual development of advanced cultures. Only through the gradual dismantling of the original humanization of everything can man become aware of his particular nature. The problem of humanity as it really is cannot be dealt with in a world view where the human is all-encompassing and man sees only human traits as his counterpart in nature. This becomes possible only when human nature is delimited within its own sphere and contrasts with the nonhuman as something specific.

Ethnocentricity and Its Conquest: The Discovery of "Humanity"

A further characteristic of earlier human self-interpretation is that very frequently recognition as a man is made conditional upon membership in one's own nation. As closely related as early peoples feel with the animals, they are far from identifying so comprehensively with their own kind. Even in cultures as advanced as the Egyptian, the privilege of being a man was reserved to Egyptians alone. All strangers were not "men." This phenomenon is called ethnocentricity. Ethnocentricity stems, on the one hand, from the fact that, originally, complex observation always outweighs selective abstraction. As early languages know only different trees but not yet the tree in general, so they know only particular nations but still have no comprehensive term for man as such. The nations differ so greatly in appearance, language, and customs that a certain degree of abstraction is necessary even to recognize that despite all differences they all belong together in what is universally human.[2]

Furthermore, all men have a tendency to revere only themselves and their own kind and conversely to look down upon strangers. At the heart of human nature is narcissistic self-love. In modern times, under the influence of an opposing ethos that enjoins us to fight against these tendencies we usually do not like to admit this. But when Homer has Odysseus declare, "I am proud to be Odysseus," then archaic man's pride in himself is still quite naïvely expressed. And when the law of Moses (Lev. 19:18) urges us to love our neighbor as ourself, it presupposes self-love as a natural fact and wants to add love of neighbor to it. Just as it extends to one's own self, self-love also extends to one's own kind. Nothing is considered higher than to preserve and, if possible, intensify this racial character. Some peoples with low foreheads therefore even artificially flatten the brows of their children still more. Anything that belongs to us is as such more valuable and superior to anything else. Someone else's ways are always inferior compared with our own. The stranger is in his difference not only ugly —for a Mongolian nothing is more repulsive than blue eyes— but he is also morally contemptible, coarse, superstitious, lawless, cruel, inhospitable, treacherous, gluttonous, and materialistic. What grounds, then, would one have to fraternize with the despised stranger under the common term "man"?

The attempt has been made to trace this contempt for the stranger back to the fact that in primitive conditions the stranger was the enemy (guest=*hostis*) against whom one had to be on guard. It is distrust and hatred for the enemy that cause us to heap all sorts of evil suspicions on him. Even during the last war both sides in their propaganda did not leave much room for humanity in their opponents. Perhaps another motive is even more deeply rooted: self-love itself experiences a justification and intensification through a feeling of superiority over another, and therefore it has an interest in disparaging him. In this desire to feel superior Sartre discovered a taproot of anti-Semitism. Finally, modern psychology has unearthed a subconscious mechanism by which each person transfers to another man or group of men—Jews, Russians, Germans, or capitalists—the bad qualities which he is vaguely aware of having himself. He projects his own evil onto others, and now he can hate it in them, while using them as a foil against which to stand out as pure and good in his own eyes. Advocates of reconciliation between nations, religions, and classes have not seen clearly enough that hatred brings an internal reward, for it comes, as it were, from a psychic deception of oneself, and that it can therefore be encountered only by seeing through this deceit and educating men to honesty toward themselves.

The belief of many nations (Jews, Romans, Russians, Germans, Americans) that they are "the chosen people" with a divine mission to dominate other nations and bring salvation to them can be regarded as a late form of ethnocentrism.

The question whether other nations are also men was discussed in the Western world only a few centuries ago, with the difference that here not membership in a certain nation but rather in a religion, namely, Christianity, was set up as the criterion for being a man. Non-Christians were formerly suspected of being creatures of the devil. Hence the astonishment of the crusaders when they arrived in the Mohammedan Orient and discovered there a culture higher than their own. For the Middle Ages only the "Christian man"—an expression still familiar from Luther—was really a man in the full sense of the word. (The Mohammedans on the other hand spoke of "Christian dogs.") Even today when an Italian wagoner strikes his donkey, he may justify himself by saying: *"Non è christiano!"* The donkey is not a Christian and therefore—not because he is not a man—one may beat him.

When with the discovery of the new world the question whether the natives were men became ever more urgent, a bull

of Pope Paul III of the year 1537 actually did state that the
Indians were "real men" (*veri homines*), but it character-
istically added "capable of receiving the Catholic faith and
sacraments" (*fidei catholicae et sacramentorum capaces*). To
be human is accordingly regarded by this document as a mere
precondition for being a Christian, and humanity finds its true
fulfillment only in this. As late as the eighteenth century, arguments were exchanged for and against the humanity of the
Indians. Though the insight into the fact that they are men
finally won out, it is typical that it took a long time to do so.
The Conquistadores themselves looked upon the Indians as
monsters whose destruction was pleasing to God. The unusually strange customs of the aborigines also seemed to the
clergymen of those times who traveled along to the New
World to be only irrational "idolatry"; and their reports to
Europe about the nakedness of the Indians, their human sac-
rifices, torture stakes, and cannibalism, contributed to the picture of the "savage" that then became current throughout
Europe for a long time. Even Hobbes, under the influence of
such missionary reports, depicted the original state of man as
a brutal war of all against all (*bellum omnium contra omnes*),
in which the sentence "Man is a wolf toward man" (*homo
homini lupus*) applies.

The Example of the Greeks

Even for the Greeks[3] the stranger is primarily a "barbarian"
(i.e., an incomprehensible stutterer; cf. the Slavic *niemicz,*
"dumb," or "German"). However, Homer did not yet know
this word. He still describes the Trojan enemy as thoroughly
noble. Only after Homer did the Greeks begin to look upon
foreign peoples as barbarians in the pejorative sense of the
word that still clings to it down to our time. In addition to
the other motives that have led all nations to despise the
stranger, the Greeks also had the institution of slavery; the

stranger was known primarily as a slave—and certainly the slave must in many cases have been degenerate because of his social position, which deprived him of all rights. Later there was added the memory of the murdering and plundering Persians. Plato in the *Protagoras* tells of a comedy writer who had presented the immorality of a wild imaginary nation on the stage. The Greek sense of superiority over the barbarians went so far that Aelian claimed that even the animals could smell the difference, for the temple dogs used to wag their tails for the Greeks, whereas they barked at the barbarians.

This archaic conception is still found anachronistically in Aristotle. As he expounds in his *Politics,* the establishment of slavery is based on nature and is necessary, for no household, not to speak of a state, can exist without it. But slavery is also justified intrinsically, for some men are suited only for coarse assignments and therefore are by nature destined to serve. They are "born slaves." That they are ruled by superiors is even fortunate for them, just as domestic animals prosper only under the rule of men. Superior men are to the slaves as the soul to the body.

Thus Aristotle tries to justify the ancient slave economy by dividing men "by nature" into masters and slaves. Indeed this difference between men even coincides broadly with the difference between Greeks and barbarians. The Greeks are by nature destined to rule, the barbarians to be slaves. Therefore, according to Aristotle, a war waged by the Greeks to subjugate the barbarians is a just war. But should the barbarians win and make slaves of the Greeks, then that is a reversal of the natural order. When his former pupil, Alexander the Great, set out to conquer Asia, Aristotle advised him to be a leader of the Greeks but a tyrant to the barbarians and to deal with them as with animals or plants. Alexander did not follow his teacher's advice, but strove for a fusion of the two cultures. A generation earlier Isocrates had given more humane advice to his father Philip than Aristotle gave to Alexander.

From the fifth century on, the empiricism of the Greek historians and writers of travel accounts, as well as Greek philosophy, militated against the prejudice of the "barbarians."
The Greeks had, as Jacob Burckhardt praised in them, "an eye
for comparing nations." Herodotus was the first to travel to
far-off lands for the express purpose of getting to know their
peoples and their history. He had himself initiated by Egyptian
priests and Persian Magi into their lore and he knew that nations such as the Egyptians, Babylonians, Phoenicians, and
Indians had developed high cultures long before the Greeks.
He admired the orderly political systems of many Orientals; in
others he praised the beautiful simplicity of their way of life,
which the Greeks had lost, much as Tacitus later, with a
culture-critical intent, contrasted the naturalness of the Ger-
manic tribes with the decadent hypercivilization of the Romans. In his cosmopolitanism Herodotus was already affected
by the Ionian enlightenment and Sophistic relativity. From
the Egyptians he also learned that they have a word in their
language corresponding exactly to the Greek "barbarian"; the
relativity of such a concept impressed him (*History* 2. 158).

How unjustified it is to always set up one's own mores as
absolute and to measure others by them he illustrated with
the following anecdote (*History* 3. 38): The Persian king
Darius asked the Hellenes who were staying at his court, for
what price they would eat the corpses of their fathers instead
of cremating them. They answered: not for any price. Then
Darius, in the presence of the Greeks, asked members of an
Indian clan for which the eating of parental corpses was cus-
tomary, for what price they would permit their dead fathers
to be burned. They shouted with horror and begged him not
even to speak of such a thing. Herodotus adds a remark about
how right Pindar was when he said that *nomos* ("custom,"
"tradition," "convention") governs everything.

Thucydides, too, did not believe in a natural difference
between the Greeks and the barbarians. The Greeks had a

higher culture, but that was only because they had reached a higher stage of development that could in principle also be reached by others (*History* 1. 5 ff.). As a proof that the difference lies only in degrees of development he used the fact that the Greeks of preclassical times resembled the contemporary barbarians in many ways: they too practiced piracy and always carried their weapons.

The physician Hippocrates summed up the difference otherwise. In his work on the influence of air, water, and earth he states that the character, mores, and mental alertness of peoples depend on the climatic and geographical conditions under which they live. Thus he is the first theoretician of climate. His theory was later taken up again by the Stoic Posidonius, and in modern times it was promulgated again by Montesquieu. This theory of climate contradicts the older view of the natural difference between the Greeks and the barbarians: only the external conditions of life bring about the respective particularities of a race. Among these conditions, however, Hippocrates includes the political: under despotism Greeks as well as barbarians become unmilitary. The same influences, therefore, produce the same habits even across the dividing line between Hellenes and barbarians.

But the Sophists were the first to proclaim as a fundamental principle the equality of all men as men. "By nature" we are all "related with one another" and "fellow citizens," says Hippias. "For each being is related by nature with those similar to it, but *Nomos* ["convention"], that tyrant of men, enforces many things contrary to nature." And Antiphon says: "For by nature we are all in every respect equal, whether barbarians or Hellenes." More decisive than the differences between peoples is the common fact of being men. Therefore a man ought to be respected as a man everywhere. He ought not to feel at home only among his own people; as a cosmopolitan, he should feel at home everywhere. "The homeland of a good soul is the entire world" (Democritus). This principle also undermines the intrinsic basis for slavery: "God created all men free, nature intended no one to be a slave" (Alcidamas).

Plato himself, though inclined by nature and origin to be conservative, nonetheless rejects the division of mankind into Greeks and barbarians even by logical analysis (*The Statesman* 262 ff.). For the concept of "the barbarians" has been coined only as a counterpart to the concept of "the Greeks." Objectively, however, there is no justification for combining the barbarians in a unified species, for there is a boundless number of barbarians of all imaginable types that have nothing in common and do not even speak the same languages. It is therefore an impermissible conceptualization to contrast the totality of non-Grecian peoples as barbarians with the one nation of the Greeks. Both the barbarians and the Greeks are only subdivisions of the more comprehensive concept "man."

But even from the earliest times a diametrically opposite stream of valuation existed concurrently with contempt for the barbarians; idealization of other peoples existed simultaneously with depiction of them as barbarians. One believes that the purity and happiness of life that one senses to be painfully lacking oneself exists among other, legendary peoples who either lived far off in time—i.e., long ago in a "golden age"—or live far off in space (even politically the tendency is to be more friendly with slightly remote countries rather than with directly adjacent neighbors). Homer had praised the piety of the Ethiopians, "who live the farthest of all nations of the earth," and the excellence of the milk-eating Hippomolgians ("mare-milkers") and the justice of the Albians, the "divinely beloved southern people." Since Homer was the bible of the Greeks, these idealized depictions still survived even when later ethnologists brought back completely contradictory reports of the coarseness, wildness, laziness, and alcoholism of these peoples. Of course, as knowledge of the world was gained, the ideal zone had to be pushed farther

back: the Scythians in the north were replaced by the Hyper-
boreans, the Ethiopians in the south by the Antipodes, the
Indians in the east by the Sereans (Chinese).

This tendency to idealize also gained adherence among the
philosophers: it can be found in the cultural policy of the
Cynics. Like Rousseau later, the Cynics opposed the excessive
cultural refinement and effeminacy of their time. Prometheus,
praised by others for bringing culture to mankind, only got
what he deserved when he was chained to a rock; Rousseau
later quoted this word for word. And as Rousseau, seeking
to break out of the modern hyperculture, set up the once-
despised "natural man" as an ideal, so in the eyes of the
Cynics the very freedom of the barbarians from the bonds
of culture made them seem worthy of emulation. Their simple
life, free of unnecessary wants, suited the Cynic ideal of
asceticism. Cynic authors therefore revived the legendary fig-
ure of the wise Scythian Anacharsis, of whom even Herodotus
reports that he had traveled to many countries. But whereas
in Herodotus the Scythian learns from his travels abroad, in
the writings of the Cynics he subjects Greek institutions to
satirical criticism and shows by contrast that the mores of
his own people are closer to nature than those of the Greeks.

In late antiquity, valuation often shifted completely in
favor of foreign countries. Non-Hellenic wisdom is placed
higher than Hellenic. As early as 400 B.C., Ctesias of Cnidos
praises the conservative stability of Chaldean philosophy compared with the contradictory divisiveness of the Greek. Later
it was even believed that the sources of Greek philosophy lay
in the East; the Greek philosophers had borrowed from Egyptian priests, Persian Magi, Indian Brahmans and gymnos-
ophists, and Babylonian Chaldeans. So attempts were made
to ennoble one's own ideas by tracing them back to far-off
times and places, and at the same time the Imperial period,
losing much that the classical times had gained, was flooded
by a wave of Eastern ideology and religion.

Although the old categorization of mankind as Greeks or

barbarians was undermined by this, it still managed to survive because since the fourth century A.D. it was given a new, internal, spiritualized meaning. Thus Isocrates, in his *Panegyric*, explains that the name "Hellene" was no longer so much a designation of national origin as of mentality: all men who participate in Hellenistic culture are called Hellenes.[4] (In the same manner Fichte was later to extend the concept of "German.") Similarly Aristotle reports that in Asia Minor he met a Jew who was a Greek not only in language but also in soul. The Stoics, too, taught that there were both bad Greeks and educated barbarians, and that therefore it was much more sensible to designate all bad men as barbarians regardless of which people they belonged to. The word "barbarian" is still used today in this sense. And accordingly the Stoics believed that the barbarians of every race were matched by a spiritual community of all men who obeyed the laws of reason, regardless of what nation they belonged to; all such men were members of the same race.

The Romans then invented a new concept for the community of higher men that existed within all peoples. On the occasion of an embassy sent by Athens to Rome in 147 B.C., the Stoic Panaetius, who was a member of it, had won the younger Scipio to the ideas of Stoic philosophy. And in the circles around Scipio there now appeared a new word which, though inspired by Greek philosophy, seems to have been coined by the Romans themselves: *humanitas*. At first it was just a fashionable term. Jurists, including Julius Caesar, avoided it as too pompous. But the stylist Cicero took it up, and it became famous primarily through him. To the more political and military, old Roman ideal of the Roman man (*homo romanus*) Cicero opposes the new ideal of man in his dignity as a man (*homo humanus*); likewise the no longer acceptable counterterm "barbarian" is replaced by the word *inhumanus*. *Humanitas* is the development and refinement of the highest moral and intellectual capabilities of man. It includes within its connotation a certain respect for one's fellowman (cf. Terence's *homo sum, humani nil a me alienum puto,* "I am a man, nothing human is strange to me," i.e., "I am concerned for the fate of other men"), also an understanding of philosophy and art and education in general, indeed even scholarship. *Humanitas,* the ennobling of one's own nature, was attainable by the Romans only through the acceptance of Greek culture by reading Greek authors, and therefore the Romans are also the first "humanists," aiming for intellectual benefits from the study of classical works.

However, the term "humanism" came into existence only at the transition to the modern era and was first derived from the *studia humaniora* (liberal arts), as contrasted with the *studia divina* (theology). These humane studies included Roman literature, which meanwhile had in turn become classical. And whereas in the Middle Ages the concept of *humanitas* had designated only human weaknesses (proneness to error, sexuality), now the Roman *humanitas* ideal came to the fore. As opposed to the ascetic ideals of Christianity the model of classical antiquity again led to a striving for an all-around development of the energies of the personality.[5]

Humanitas too was limited in its scope and not ascribed to all men. It stood in contrast to *"inhumanitas."* Now the boundary between the respected and the despised individual no longer corresponded with the boundary between one's own people and foreign nations, but as before a chasm still split humanity. Not all men satisfied the ideal of *humanitas.* Still, it is very significant that this ideal was called *humanitas* at all. For this connotes that the ideal consists only in the development of man's true nature. In principle this is accessible to all men, because everyone has it intrinsically by virtue of being a man.

This ideal of humanity, then, brings a further advantage, namely, that mankind as a whole becomes a unity. One nation is no longer contrasted with all others as something totally heterogeneous, but there is—corresponding to the reality of the Hellenized Mediterranean world and the Roman Empire[6]

—one mankind.[7] Though one person or group may be superior
to the other because it better represents the ideal of humanity,
still it remains linked with all the others by the fact that each
participates in the same idea and contains potentially the
same perfection.

In a completely different manner than the Greeks and
Romans, the third classical people of antiquity, the Jews, also
made a breakthrough to the idea of one humanity. For the
Jews this was a consequence of their monotheism: if there
is only one God, then he is the God of all men, who are thereby
brought closer together as children of God. And since God
was at the same time understood to be the director of history,
another consequence followed which was later developed
still further in Christianity: i.e., mankind, which is directed
by God toward a common goal, also has a common destiny;
there is such a thing as "world history." For the Greeks, each
individual nation had its own special history, and these separate histories were not subsumed into a higher unity. Objectively the Greeks were right, because world history in the true
sense of the word begins only in our century. Still, the Judeo-
Christian idea of a divinely guided history of all mankind
must be considered of value because this religious shell contained the seed of the stronger knowledge that all mankind
belongs together.

Ethnocentricity Since the Eighteenth Century

Like antiquity, the eighteenth century—rather than maintaining the older image of the "savages"—is enthusiastic for
the "natural peoples," as they were then called, and considers
them purer and nobler than "Europe's veneer of courtliness."

> Behold, you wise white people,
> Behold, we savages are the better men.
> (Seume)

Already Montaigne had glorified the "good savage," and the Jesuit Lafitau, one of the most widely read travel authors of his time, reported in 1724 on the mores of the American aborigines and expressly contradicted authors who depicted the natives as creatures without culture, law, or God, "who have almost no human characteristics except the external shape." Led partly by the Pelagianism rampant in his Order and partly by the principles of the Enlightenment, which made it possible to regard other religions not only as idolatry but as other real religions, his eyes were open for the humanly valuable qualities of the native. Rousseau in his *Discours sur l'origine et le fondement de l'inégalité parmi les hommes* (1755) then deduced from Lafitau's data his idea of equating civilization with the fall of man—"all is well when it issues from the hand of the author of things; but everything degenerates in the hands of men"—for he believed that the natural customs to which he wanted to return still existed among the non-European peoples. The myth of the idyllic natural man also provided him with a utopian standard by which his political and social criticism could castigate the conditions of European society, and also introduce a bucolic and sentimental view of nature.[8]

But the eighteenth century's knowledge is not limited to a general enthusiasm for natural man; it also develops anew the ideal of one indivisible mankind ("humanity" becomes a pathos-laden slogan of the time) in which "all men are brothers" (Schiller). In fact, this idea is arrived at by two opposite lines of thought.

First, the men of the Enlightenment come forward with the thesis that though mankind is indeed divided into different nations with different religions, these differences are only accidental, and essentially man is always and everywhere the same. Beneath the surface of nationally and religiously particularized men one always discovers the universal man; and precisely what we have in common with all other men is the only thing of value in us. Therefore the nations should make peace with one another and religions should be tolerant. For everything that separates us is only secondary. Indeed, ultimately the multiplicity of peoples and religious confessions must be regarded not only as secondary but even as merely temporary; their very multiplicity is a proof that the ideal of universal man dormant in all of us is reflected only imperfectly in the various nations and has not yet developed to its full perfection. From this ensues the mission of finally casting aside all particularity and creating the one human culture that corresponds to the idea of one mankind and is identical for all men. Therefore also one world language should replace the many national tongues.

This point of view, which is still widespread in the Western world, was superseded especially in Germany by an opposite opinion which saw the fact of belonging to a particular nation not as something superficial but as a factor that shaped man through and through. Substantially and in every fiber of his being he is a representative of this people and this is by no means regrettable; in fact, it is the best thing about him. The universal man whom the thinkers of the Enlightenment thought they had discovered does not exist at all. It is absolutely impossible to be just a man; one must of necessity be black or white, man or woman, child or adult, etc. The concept of man is realized and fulfilled only within such closer specifications.

With this theory the Goethe period (Goethe was active as a writer 1772–1832) still stands squarely within the scope of the Enlightenment, for, with the Enlightenment, it does not, as was earlier the case, elevate one single nation—one's own —above all others. It too in principle gives all nations the same rank. But its reason for doing so is new and different; it does this not because it considers the difference between one nation and another irrelevant, as the Enlightenment did, but quite the contrary: every nation maintains its rank only by virtue of its specific national character.

Is this not a betrayal of the faith in the intrinsic unity of all mankind? Once again the nations seem to differ radically one from the other; no connecting bond between them seems apparent. Modern nationalism and dogmatic ideologies seem to have one of their roots in this—"from humanity, via nationality, to bestiality" (Grillparzer). And yet the connecting bond is discoverable as soon as one reflects that unity does not need to consist in the homogeneity and uniformity of all members. Each nation and age is a necessary instrument in the orchestra of mankind, a fully equal and valuable component that contributes to the perfection of corporate humanity. Just as for the philosophers Nicholas of Cusa and Leibniz the world is individuated at every point so that not one particle of dust resembles another, but each one reflects the whole world in its own way (*in omnibus partibus relucet totum*) and each one has its irreplaceable position within the cosmic structure, so according to Herder and the Romantics on the level of the history of philosophy each nation gives expression to humanity in its distinctive manner, and each expression is in its own way the entirety, yet all together are required for the adequate expression of all mankind. "The human," says Goethe, "needs all men for its realization; the true man can exist only by virtue of all mankind."

Therefore it is an error for the individual to suppress his specific characteristics in favor of a universal concept of man, for instance. He ought to become aware of his own nature and foster it. Only this gives man a taste for life. But at the same time he should realize that his nature is only one among countless others with equal rights and that the common humanity is also manifested in the particularities of others. The theorists of the Enlightenment demand tolerance because all men are basically alike and the differences do not count; Herder and the Romantics demand it because man's most precious heritage resides precisely in the differences among men and each one ought to honor in other beings other priceless beauty and meaning that he would not want to do without.

Indeed, one ought not merely to honor other beings for what they are but also to open oneself to them with understanding and contemplate them lovingly. Since each one in his own existence represents only one particular aspect of mankind, he ought to complement himself by internal acceptance of other beings. For Humboldt, knowledgeable participation in others is the highest postulate of education. Through universality to totality! Thus he deepened the older humanism, which sought to gain refinement and urbanity by contact with classical antiquity. This method of education is based on a "sense of history" that was also beginning to form at that time. Whoever despises someone else has no reason to bother more closely about him. But the Enlightenment man too has no reason to do so, because though he does value the other person it is not precisely for his differences but because he also discovers universal man in him. Only the Goethe period values and therefore seeks out what is different precisely because it is different. The historical and cultural modifications of what it means to be a man are then no longer just so many imperfect attempts at realizing one single idea of man; rather, they exhaust the fullness of humanity only in their concrete multiplicity. They are therefore much more enlightening for the nature of man than a mere rational definition. Christianity had used a similar line of argumentation against Greek thought when it claimed that men are intrinsically different depending on whether they lived before or after Christ and that therefore it is not enough to know the timeless idea of man, which is more determinable in its historicity. This reasoning is taken up and formalized during the Goethe period. Whoever wants to learn about the nature of man must consult not the philosophers but the historians. And what is true of man is true of his institutions. Whether it is the state, religion, or philosophy, it cannot be properly understood only by rational analysis. Direct observation of the phenomenon in the multiplicity of its historical variations is also necessary.

By "humanity," the eighteenth century meant not only the fact of universal humanity and the factual unity of the human race but a value and an ideal to be aimed for. Already when Diogenes the Cynic lighted a lantern in the marketplace of Athens to look, as he said, for a man, he was playing with the double meaning of the word, with its upper and lower range of meaning. Likewise Menander, in his famous verse: "What a delightful thing is man, when he is a man." So Lessing's *Nathan der Weise*:

> . . . are we
> Our people? What does that mean, "people"?
> Are Christian and Jew Christian and Jew
> Before they are men? Ah! if only I had found one counterpart
> Among you, who considered it enough
> To be called a man!

When Nathan so speaks, the pathos is already a sign that "man" here is not merely a general term that is left over when one abstracts from the national and religious characteristics of each individual. That the impulse was felt here to shake off all particularities as limitations and to grow beyond them in order to be nothing but man stems only from the fact that "man" here was advanced as an ethical postulate full of content.[9]

The same is true of the adjective "human," though it also gains a narrower meaning in the variant "humane." A person acts "humanely"—in contrast with the inhuman beast and the bestial and brutal cruelty otherwise prevalent in nature —when he spares the weak, helps those in need, and, generally, when he not only sees and asserts himself but when he is sensitive to the rights and desires of his fellowman and also honors man in the sick and destitute (cf. "philanthropy"). Where such help is organized, the adjective "humanitarian" is used.

But the abstract noun "humanity" retained the broader meaning of *humanitas,* and the two terms "man" and "humanity" had their heyday in the eighteenth century. No one loved the word "humanity" as did Herder (cf. his "Letters for the Promotion of Humanity"); therefore Goethe intended to memorialize him with the title "humanus" in his *Geheimnisse* ("Secrets"), which remained incomplete. When Herder attempted to translate *"humanitas,"* the linguistically equivalent *Menschlichkeit* turned out to be too narrow. Gellius had already known that *humanitas* is not merely philanthropy; he therefore employed the word *paideia*. Herder translates *humanitas* as *Menschheit*. Thereby *Menschheit* acquires a double meaning—which Herder welcomed. When he called his masterpiece *Ideen zur Philosophie der Geschichte der Menschheit* ("Ideas for a Philosophy of the History of Humanity"), this title meant for him not only the external history of actual mankind. Humanity, for him, also means the quintessence of human perfection, and this perfection also happens to have a history; it undergoes development both for the individual and for mankind as a whole. The capacity for humanity is innate by the very fact of being a man, but the human must grow to maturity. We are basically not yet true men but still have to become so. Anthropology is achieved by means of the history of philosophy.

CHAPTER 3

Selected Data Toward
a History of Anthropology

The Fifth Century B.C.

According to a famous formulation by Cicero, Socrates is said
to have brought philosophy from heaven down to earth. For
the so-called pre-Socratic philosophy had been predominantly
"natural philosophy," that is, cosmological metaphysics. Socrates, on the other hand, was the first pure ethician; his only
concern was the inner world of man. The old inscription on
the temple of Apollo at Delphi, "Know thyself" (i.e., know
that you are a man and not God), he interpreted in the new,
more internal sense that man ought to listen inwardly and
lift unknown treasures out of his own depths (cf. Heraclitus'
earlier "I investigated myself"). Through Plato, Socrates' initiative was to influence world history. His doctrines of the dualism of body and soul, of the otherworldly homeland of the
soul for which it longs from its earthly prison, of the pre-
dominance of the rational in it, by which it also ought to
conquer the desires that rise up out of the body—all this
has been engraved indelibly into the self-understanding of
subsequent humanity.

Nonetheless, the merit of having introduced a sort of "anthropological era" in antiquity belongs not to Socrates but to
the so-called Sophists. Attic regional pride may have played a
part when Socrates as the true philosopher was so sharply

contrasted with the contemporary Ionian Sophists (the word still has a bad taste). Compared with previous philosophers, Socrates should really be classified together with the Sophists, and in his focus on man he is actually dependent on them. But whereas Socrates discovered man under the perspective of ethics, the Sophists discovered him under the perspective of cultural philosophy. They are also the first philosophers of cultural philosophy. They are the first anthropologists because they are also the first philosophers of culture. How much anthropology and cultural philosophy overlap we have already seen in the introductory remarks: man is the being that must decide on his living arrangements himself, and this aspect of self-determination is what we call culture. But though this is a fact, man is generally not aware of it. Originally the nations believed that their cultural institutions either were given by nature or were a gift of the gods. Every nation considers its institutions absolutely necessary and right; it assumes that precisely these and no others are anchored in the nature of things.

The Sophists, on the other hand, employing a pair of contrary concepts which they made famous,[1] proclaim that our cultural institutions, especially our customs and laws, are not given by nature (*physei*) but stem from human convention (*nomō* and *thesei*). As a proof of this they point to the ethnological evidence that was being gathered in abundance at that time. The multiplicity of human institutions is so tremendous that it would be impossible to assume that all other nations had false customs and only one's own were prescribed by nature. The conclusion that can be drawn from this multiplicity is, on the contrary, that obviously no customs whatever are prescribed by nature. But this is not a purely negative statement; it implies the converse, namely, that man may legitimately invent and create customs for himself. Thus for the first time man's power to create culture is revealed and man is recognized and celebrated as the creative center. He is the one who can establish a norm (*nomos*).

Aeschylus in his *Prometheus* had described how the benefi-
cent Titan brought not only fire to men, who were still completely uncultured, but also the arts of constructing houses,
manufacturing containers, and all the beginnings of culture.
A few decades later, however, the famous chorus from Sopho-
cles' *Antigone,* which gave poetical expression to the newly
acquired image of man, says: "Many mighty beings exist, but
nothing is mightier than man." And then an enumeration is
made of how man does not obtain his cultural institutions
through a higher grace but produces them by the power of
his own spirit. Navigation, agriculture, hunting, the taming
of domestic animals, language, wisdom, weaponry, cities, all
this is his own creation. He himself is Prometheus.

The conventionality of human culture is subject to various
interpretations. One can approve convention, as Democritus
did. One can reject conventions as mere conventions and yet
still desire to penetrate through to true nature (*physis*), or
—and this further development of the doctrine is considered
specifically "Sophistic"—one can conclude: if man can produce
his mores himself and choose any of the most varied types,
then all mores are only arbitrary creations that can be replaced by other arbitrary creations. In that case the individual no longer need respect the mores considered valid
within his circle, but each can at any time determine for himself what he wants to consider good and valid. This carrying
of the idea of creativity to the extreme of mere creative arbitrariness was what gave virulence to the opposition against the
Sophists and led Plato to teach eternal, preexistent norms that
man must recognize and merely carry out in thought and deed.
This eliminated the element of arbitrariness from our actions,
but it also caused the creative element that the Sophists had
discovered to be lost sight of.

The Sophist Protagoras associated man's ability to create
culture with his bodily constitution. In the Platonic dialogue
named after him he states, in mythical form, that man is very
badly equipped compared with the beasts: nature has given

him neither organs for flight nor organs for attack, no protective fur, no claws, etc., and his senses are less sharp than those of animals. How then does man manage to assert himself in life? Later the Cynics added to this: nature has destined man for a life of abstinence. It is only because we are spoiled by a hundred cultural conveniences which we have created for ourselves, that we no longer can imagine how men earlier could live without these conveniences. But they could very well, and therefore we too should give up the unnatural and useless luxury of our civilized state and return to the hardiness and simplicity of the primeval condition. Protagoras took a completely different line of argument. That man disposes over technical and moral energies, that he can call the arts of Hephaestus (metallurgy) and Athena (agriculture) as well as shame and law his own is the necessary compensation for his physical weakness. Through these cultural forces he makes up for what the animals surpass him in by the perfection of their organs and their instincts. Indeed, as often "the last are first," he even surpasses them: the one who first seemed to have been left empty-handed is most richly compensated. Diogenes of Apollonia saw the physical and intellectual constitutions as interlapping in another way, but for him man's intellect was not merely a compensation for his physical shortcomings, but man was from the start favored by his upright gait, his tongue (language), and his hands.

The Sophists also applied their theory of man's creativity to epistemology. Not only our institutions but even our truths are shown under closer examination to be our own creations. Every unreflected opinion assumes that things really are as presented to our senses and our thought. We consider wine sweet because it tastes sweet. Knowledge seems merely to depict things as they really are in the world outside. On the contrary, the pre-Socratics, and the Sophists after them, had discovered that the sweetness of wine is only a *pros ti*, relative to the subjective equipment of our senses. Wine seems to be sweet only because our tongue reacts so to it; but how it is of itself, we do not know. Proof: it seems sweet only to the healthy person, but bitter to the sick man. Not that only one person is right while the others are wrong; in principle the Sophist considered all apparent truth in which we move to be conditioned by our subjective constitution. Knowledge does not depict a world that exists independently of us, but it automatically constructs a subjective human world corresponding to our organization; indeed, within the world of man it places each person inside an individual subjective world of his own.

Previously Parmenides had concluded from a direct metaphysical experience that the world of our senses is only a deception. But Parmenides still believed that behind this deception a world as such exists and is accessible to our knowledge. Our senses falsify it but it reveals itself to our reason. Just as his fellow Eleatic, Xenophanes, sees through the anthropomorphism of the Homeric Olympus, which is structured by analogy with our human conditions, so Parmenides sees that our entire world of perception is dependent on man and the subjectivity of his senses. And just as Xenophanes wants to eradicate anthropomorphism and introduce a more spiritual concept of God, so Parmenides wants to shatter the deception of the senses and penetrate mentally to true reality.

The Sophists eliminate this metaphysical substructure posited by Parmenides. Beyond the phenomenon there is nothing more real (neither knowable nor unknowable); the phenomenon itself is ultimate. And since it is ultimate it is not, as for Parmenides, based merely on an involuntary falsification or distortion of reality, that is, on a defect, but like culture it is a product of positive invention or creation. This theory, which sets the phenomenal world relative to men as absolute, is called phenomenalism (cf. Nietzsche), or also anthropocentrism or hominism. It was expressed pragmatically by Protagoras in his famous sentence *"anthrōpos metron pantōn,"* man —and this applies both to the species and the individual—is the measure of all things, of the existent that they may be, and of the nonexistent that they may not be. Protagoras does not seek to undo the dependence of the world we perceive on our perception itself. It is inevitable; nor is it to be regretted but rather affirmed. Since nothing is left by which to measure and test our perceptions, they become reality, and their only criterion is the man who sees them. Yet this is not due to an inadequacy on man's part; on the contrary, he can feel proud to be the center of the world. By this line of reasoning, the Sophists—unfortunately supplanted by Platonism, which became totally predominant—were early precursors of the modern age.

The Modern Age

After the many centuries of the Middle Ages, which had a primarily transcendental orientation, man was rediscovered only upon the rediscovery of the secular realm in general by the Renaissance. The Renaissance strove to understand man no longer from within the framework of religion or from God's point of view, but immanently, as he is in himself (Dilthey). Christian mysticism had prepared the way by describing man's inner states and experiences, but now "the content of human nature itself" (Dilthey) was being investigated on a broader basis. The first and for a long time the most significant philosophical anthropology that embodied the feelings of the new era is that of the young Pico della Mirandola, *De hominis dignitate*, published in 1486. But this promising beginning of the Renaissance had only a scanty following, since after Descartes interest no longer focused on man but on consciousness. Only thinkers who expressly took a stand outside the Cartesian line still had a feeling for anthropology. Among the best of these independent thinkers are Pascal and Herder and the Goethe period in general, on which the nineteenth century then built. The main interest of the so-called French moralists, e.g., Montaigne, La Rochefoucauld, remains ethical and psychological, and that of the English remains political and sociological in nature. Pope justified the new turning to man in "An Essay on Man" (1733) with the famous sentence (which could already be found in Charron): "The proper study of mankind is man," or as Goethe once put it: "For man the most interesting thing is man." At a more recent time the term "anthropology" gained some currency because Kant in 1798 wrote a work of his old age under that title.

In his lectures on logic Kant once proposed an impressive program, viz., that the three main questions of epistemology, ethics, and theology, *What can I know? What should I do? What hope may I have?* could be summed up in one question: *What is man?* In his book *Kant and the Problem of Metaphysics*, which is completely off the track as an interpretation of the historical Kant, Heidegger used this as his point of departure, believing that he could use a return to Kant as authorization to make the existence of man the starting point of his own philosophy. According to Martin Buber's more correct interpretation, Kant believed that these so different questions were interlinked in man only because he participated in both the finite and the infinite.

The anthropology which Kant then wrote did not meet his own high standards, nor did it attempt to. It is only a descriptive, ethnological, and psychological anthropology full of curiosities. In its very title Kant calls it an anthropology "in a pragmatic sense": it is not intended to present academic doctrines from school and for school but from the world for the world. In quaint professional jargon the reader is advised: "He who imbibes intoxicating beverages to such an excess that he is for a time incapable of organizing his sensory perceptions according to the rules of experience is called drunk or intoxicated." We learn further that women's legs are made to look thinner by the wearing of black stockings and that seasickness is not caused by the swaying of our own body but by the fact that our sense of sight loses its firm orientation in space through the swaying of the ship. Compared with Kant's other works, this is a terribly shallow piece of writing.

Kant's more strictly philosophical interest in anthropology is exclusively ethical. "Physiological knowledge of man," he writes, "aims at research into what nature makes of man; pragmatic knowledge of man studies what he, as a free being, makes or can and should make of himself," namely, as a moral personality. Anthropology shows "the subjective conditions for carrying out the moral laws." Today, however, anthropology strives precisely for a purely anthropological viewpoint independent of ethics (and also of psychology).

But though Kant's anthropology did not meet expectations, still the mere fact that an anthropology was also listed among the great thinker's works did its part toward preventing anthropology from sinking into complete oblivion in subsequent years. Schulze, Fries, the younger Fichte, Michelet, all wrote anthropologies, often with the adjective "psychological" prefixed to "anthropology." And Lotze's anthropology by the title of *Mikrokosmos* was even, for a few decades, a standard work on the bookshelf of the educated middle-class family.

Feuerbach is the first modern philosopher who no longer wants to start with the world, nor like Hegel with the world reason, nor like Descartes and Kant with merely man's reason, but with the whole man. Man ought not to be just one topic of philosophy among others; he ought to stand right in its center. This makes Feuerbach a precursor of the current attitude. However, Feuerbach's motive was different. He proclaimed anthropology so passionately because it was to replace theology. Anthropology is the "mystery of theology." All characteristics that were formerly worshiped in God should now be recognized as primarily human traits projected by man into God and they should be returned to man, honored only in him and also intensified in him.

Feuerbach here shows a time-conditioned similarity of style with Auguste Comte, who wanted to introduce self-idolization of humanity in an even cruder form (e.g., by replacing the Christian saints with geniuses significant for their contribution to human progress). After the religious (and the metaphysical) stage of history has been overcome, one ought to set up a cult to the "great being, humanity." Swinburne was yet to write: "Glory to man in the highest." This cult of humanity, however, has a previous model in the cult of reason as the Supreme Being, which the French Revolution sought to establish.

The Present

In the 1920's an "anthropological renaissance" took place; all philosophical disciplines seemed to converge toward anthropology. With a fine sense for what seminal ideas were in the air, Max Scheler had, before World War I, written an essay, "On the Idea of Man," in which he stated: "In a certain sense all central problems of philosophy can be traced back to the question of what man is." And toward the end of his life he wrote: "If there is a philosophical task whose solution our age needs with singular desperation it is that of a philosophical anthropology. I mean a basic science on the nature and constitution of man." With a brief work called *Man's Place in the Universe,* Scheler himself also became one of the most stimulating contributors to modern German anthropology. He was making preparations for a more voluminous work. Only a posthumous edition of his unpublished writings could make the anthropological activity of his last years fully accessible.

Many roads lead to modern anthropology:

1. *The metaphysical motive.* First, positivism had separated the sciences from the broader framework of theology and metaphysics and made them autonomous and specialized individual disciplines. During the general reaction against positivism which took place in the first third of the twentieth century, anthropology again offered hope for a central discipline to cast light on the sciences and provide them with a common philosophical unity. Even within many sciences, the introduction of the anthropological viewpoint led beyond the merely

positivistic registration of facts and established a point of reference around which information about particulars could be organized.

2. *The transcendental motive.* What led many philosophers of the 1920's to anthropology was their dissatisfaction with epistemology—which had until then been monopolizing all attention—a dissatisfaction which had already found expression in *Lebensphilosophie.* Since everything is made available only by knowledge, knowledge had, since Descartes, been considered the primary fact that philosophy had to begin with. Now it was becoming evident that knowledge is only one of the functions of awareness. And awareness itself is only one part in the totality of human life. The elementary fact is therefore obviously not the knowing subject but the subject of life, man as a whole. Only from this whole can the place and meaning even of knowledge be correctly assessed. Man's universe of knowledge must relate not only to the forms of perception and categories but also to the practical aspects of human life; he is also the creator of his cultural world. Thus anthropology establishes a deeper and broader basis for transcendentalism: it traces its foundations back to their ultimate source. (The same is true of linguistic analysis. Both disciplines are modern reformulations of the question of transcendentalism.)

3. *The ontological motive.* The opposition of the 1920's criticized previous philosophy not only for beginning with epistemology but also for stopping there. For positivists and neo-Kantians had reduced philosophy almost entirely to the epistemological foundation of the sciences. The objective study of the world itself seemed to have been transferred to the sciences. In contrast, phenomenology stressed especially that philosophy also had objects of study of its own. In a counterattack against epistemological idealism, philosophy once again recalled that its basic questions are not epistemological but metaphysical.

This seemed to open the way for a "renaissance of metaphysics" and ontology. Others, however, do not want to surrender all too easily philosophy's Cartesian point of departure from the subject. Anthropology, which deals with man as a subject, not merely as a subject of knowledge but as a subject of existence, would seem in some ways to be the ideal synthesis between the modern starting point with the subject and modern trends toward metaphysics. Perhaps the being that we ourselves are is not just any, but a special region of reality both in its existence and in the access to being that it makes possible.

4. *The liberal arts (Geisteswissenschaften) motive.* In addition to philosophy, the intellectual and cultural sciences call for philosophical anthropology. Some have correctly called them "the sciences of man"; they all deal with "man in his actions and experiences" (J. Burckhardt) and his works; they have the realm of man as their subject. The deeper understanding of the soul and of culture which they have developed since the Enlightenment and the Goethe period was actually the start of an "anthropological era." But all these sciences lack a common basis and one task of philosophical anthropology would be to prepare such a common foundation for all of them, to form a discipline dealing with the basic principles of the liberal arts and sciences.

To accomplish this, it would have to synthesize and deepen the essentials in our abundant, detailed knowledge of man such as no previous age has known. Nothing is more pitiful than an unscientific philosophy that thinks it can answer all the questions by itself. But at the same time philosophy can never, as was implied by Positivism's program of an "inductive metaphysics," be limited only to the same point of departure as the sciences; it must in principle go a step beyond the sciences and gain a genuine access of its own to reality. But the objection has been made against philosophical anthropology that it is only a reaction to the sciences, that it synthesizes their empirical results but cannot provide a theoretical foundation for their field of research and methods.

5. *The ideological motive.* At its deepest root, however, the question about man stems neither from philosophy nor from the sciences but from the need of the times. Therefore, it does not remain merely academic and internal to philosophy; it is also asked by medicine and theology, by psychology and philosophy of education. In all ages when a consolidated and well-organized order of life prevails, man has a clearly defined image of himself. He thinks he knows who he is and therefore he does not need to ask about himself. But modern man, despite or perhaps precisely because he has such manifold knowledge of the world of men, lacks such a valid self-image. In addition to the religious image of man, the apparently so evident image of man as a rational being has been undermined: Schopenhauer and Marx, Nietzsche and Freud, have shown us that man is in reality moved by quite other forces than those of reason. Nietzsche especially was skilled at unmasking the artificial, apparent worlds behind which man is accustomed to hiding his true reality. So often the human turns out to be all-too-human. Morality too was just such an illusory world in which man falsely interpreted himself as a moral being. "Now we have destroyed morality—and we have again become completely dark to ourselves!" (*The Will to Power,* aphorism 594). As a substitute for the idealistically palliated images of man, the naturalistic image of man as a wise animal was then presented. But after a brief popularity this too receded. Thus all the old traditions are still familiar to us, but none of them is binding. As heirs to the great historical studies of the nineteenth century we can no longer regard any of man's historical interpretations and forms as representing his eternal essence. Man has become, as Scheler says, problematic as never before; he no longer knows what he is, and he knows that he does not know it. Unsure of his way, questionable to himself, he therefore studies with unparalleled concern his own significance and reality, where he came from and what his destination is. But when he struggles for a new self-understanding, he is also struggling for his future form. The quest

for an anthropology determines our reality. Everyone realizes
vaguely that the question of man is the question that decides
our fate.

The method of philosophical anthropology is often to start
with a noticeable human quality and ask backwards from
that: how must a being be constituted if this characteristic ful-
fills a meaningful and indispensable function in it (Bollnow)?
In other words, a deduction is made from an observed detail to the presumably still unknown entirety of man. The
phenomenon in question can be evident, such as upright gait
(Herder), fear (Kierkegaard), work (Marx), the ability to
ask questions (Löwith), the ability to depict (Jonas), or fes-
tivity (Bollnow), as well as objectivity, educability, shame. Or
it can be a scientific discovery, such as the specific nature of
human intelligence, gained from Köhler's comparison of man
with the apes (Scheler), anatomy (Gehlen), the extrauterine
year (Portmann). But cultural objectivizations can also serve
as the starting point. For Dilthey, objective culture is the
main organ of anthropology, the text by which it deciphers
the nature of its author, as he produces culture, ever differently, but with a specific style at each point in history.
Feuerbach used the mirror of religion to discover man in
his concealment—though he did so with the intention of
reductively eliminating the objectified cultural phenomenon.
But, not only the results of scientific knowledge reveal the
creative mind, but language and myth also do; thus Ernst
Cassirer established a bridge between Kantian and anthropological transcendentalism.

Anthropology and Existentialism

The same 1920's that produced anthropology also gave rise
to existentialism. It too inquires about the human condition
(a term borrowed by Malraux from Charron). But existentialism is not anthropology. How are the two interrelated?

Groethuysen says it makes a big difference whether man speaks of himself in the third or in the first person. In anthropology, man investigates what sort of particular existence and what place in the universe "he" has, along with all other entities. He observes himself, as it were, from the outside. Existentialism, however, observes him from within. It focuses on the riddle of the respective personal self and exclaims it. This self is, for it, not merely one instance of a general phenomenon. It discovers the heart of man's existence precisely in his individuality, in his temporal concreteness. Therefore its links with the Christian image of man, which centered on the fate of the individual soul, are closer than with the previous philosophical image of man. In his passion for complete realization of the self, Kierkegaard criticized Hegel for believing, in his "world-historical preoccupation," that the individual is the generation and forgetting what it means "to be a man! Not a man in general but that you and I and he, each one for himself, are men." "One becomes a man by aping others. One knows that one is a man not by that very fact but as a conclusion: one is like the others, therefore one is a man. God knows whether any one of us really is so! And in this age when everything has been and is being doubted, no one thinks of this one doubt: God knows whether any one of us is a man." As long as one has in mind only universal man, one might still say with Democritus (*Fr.* 165): man is what we all know. But with regard to one's own self the sentence has to be completely reversed: no one knows what man is. By slipping into the mask of universal man, we are too easily satisfied with merely superficial self-knowledge and in effect we are hiding from ourselves. Not unintentionally: as Nietzsche and Freud knew, man is afraid of a too-direct encounter with himself and seeks to avoid it.[2] And yet he can become genuine in his reality only if he tears off the mask of self-deception and forces himself to be completely truthful with himself.

If we examine individual thinkers, Karl Jaspers is opposed

to philosophical anthropology because anthropology would entail firm knowledge of man and make definitive statements about him. But man is the only thing in existence that offers absolutely no basis for this, because as such he has no definitive firmness. Basically man is open possibility; he has, as Bergson impressively showed, no unchangeable reality; he always retains freedom to decide about his own existence. "To be a man is to be in the process of becoming a man," is an incessant act of self-creation. Therefore "what man is cannot be ontologically determined." "Existentialism would be lost immediately if it claimed to know what man is." Anthropology is possible only for the person who fails to recognize the existential abyss in us, who sees something objectively solid where in reality creative unrest prevails. The only appropriate manner in which to speak of man is not an objectifying anthropology but "illumination of existence," which incessantly blurs the definiteness of every statement and thus lets existence shine forth indirectly, as if by a negative method. Therefore it becomes an appeal not to let our existence coagulate into supposed knowledge but rather to accept the challenge of freedom. Ultimately existence becomes accessible to us only as our existence and not merely as known, but in the living exercise of existence itself.

But apparently Jaspers is dealing with an arbitrarily narrow concept of anthropology. It is not essential for anthropology to determine man unequivocally. Why couldn't it too accept the insight into his openness and freedom of decision? Jasper's concept of the object is also too narrow. Why should objective knowledge of man's freedom be impossible?

In direct contradiction to Jaspers, Sartre proclaims, even in the title of one of his books, that he is dealing with man: *L'Existentialisme est un humanisme* ("Existentialism is a humanism"). Here humanism should not be understood as classical humanism. Humanism, for Sartre, means that conception of man whereby each one of us ought to find his source of life within himself. As was the case with Feuerbach's anthropology, Sartre's humanism too stands in strong opposition to theism: Not God creates man, but we create ourselves. Each one of us must, out of our own interior resources, decide responsibly what kind of man he wants to be. Existentialism is a humanism because it recognizes man's specific task as a lawgiver, which no other creature has, namely to discover and shape his own nature.

In Heidegger, things are more complex. For Heidegger's existentialism wants to be at the same time and even primarily an ontology. As he himself says in the introduction to *Being and Time,* he was interested primarily in the general question about the meaning of existence. But what took him from there to the analysis of human existence?

Two great types of metaphysics have been at odds for ages. On the one hand, metaphysics of the world has a great tradition dating back to the pre-Socratics and Aristotle. Its most significant representative in the first half of our century was Nicolai Hartmann. Our perception and our thinking, he taught, are by nature, in their right intention, directed not at the subject but at the outside world which the subject must know in order to be able to move in it. Our awareness is, far more, awareness of the world, rather than self-awareness. Only by interaction with the outside do we originally get to know ourselves too, and it is only an artificial inversion, an oblique intention that makes the subject its own object. Not only is other reality known earlier, it is also more easily known. We are less mistaken about it, precisely because we have more distance to it. Other than one might think, that which is closest in reality is furthest in knowledge.

According to Hartmann, who with his trend toward objectivity continues the Goethean line of German thought, man is only one link (though perhaps the most valuable) in a much greater chain of reality. We said of knowledge that, ontologically speaking, it is embedded in the entirety of human life and an understanding of it must be preceded by an understanding of man; similarly man is embedded in the greater whole of the entire world and can be understood only in this total context. Therefore, according to Hartmann, not anthropology but ontology in general must be philosophy's systematic point of departure as it was historically for the Greeks. To stop with anthropology is a half measure. What we must achieve is a breakthrough not in anthropology but in ontology. The anthropological solution is contained within the ontological one, since anthropology studies man only as one being along with others of equal rank.

In sharp contrast, the metaphysics of the self starts with man and the soul. Augustine already accused man of admiring mountain peaks, the ocean tide, and the course of the stars but "abandoning" himself and not marveling at the great mystery (*grande profundum*) of his own nature: "Do not go outside, return within yourself, truth dwells within man." This metaphysics of the self can appear with different claims. On the one hand it can seek to limit itself completely to the human and bother about nothing else; the reason being either that human existence is incomparably more valuable or at any rate the only thing that concerns us, everything else being only the background for it (this is the trend among ethically and religiously oriented minds); or that it is the only thing we can know (which we just saw to be contested by Hartmann). On the other hand the starting point with the subject can broaden out into the universal and seek to understand all reality. Just as cosmological metaphysics includes man as a part of the world, just as mysticism believes it finds God in the depths of the soul, metaphysics of the self can rise to the world. "The soul is in a certain way everything" (Aristotle). Leibniz therefore understands the world monads by analogy with our own self-monads, and Fichte and Schopenhauer also affirmed such an analogy. The most prominent spokesman for this procedure in our century was Scheler. He too appealed to Aristotle's dictum and declared that modern metaphysics ought no longer to be cosmology but meta-anthropology. This point makes Scheler the chief inspiration of Heidegger.

According to Heidegger, human existence is that being which—to use a phrase of Kierkegaard, whom Heidegger refuses to recognize as a predecessor—"has a relationship to itself": it is distinguished from all other things in that it is concerned with its own being, struggles for true existence, and has an understanding of this existence in this struggle. Existence, as Heidegger formulates it, is not only ontic but also ontological. Just as for Dilthey all life is as such hermeneutic, so according to Heidegger ontology is not a late accomplishment of philosophy but a necessity of immediate existence. And as Dilthey had recommended that philosophy appropriate the self-interpretation of life at the level where it is still untouched by speculative confusion, Heidegger does the same. That is why his ontology takes the path of an analysis of human existence.

But our existence does not always give us the right understanding of being. Very often its own true being is hidden from it by a shallow concept of being. Like Plato, Augustine, Pascal, and Kierkegaard, Heidegger knew that man lives, as it were, on two levels and constantly goes from one to the other. Habitually he lives on the level of "nongenuineness": with derived and false concepts of everyday life such as are insinuated to him by the "chatter" of "people," he obstructs his most innate possibilities. He plays the role that the surrounding world expects of him. One experience above all, anxiety, which in its purest form is fear of death, lifts me up to the level of "genuineness" on which I recognize and decisively take up my own individual destiny.

Therefore Heidegger's descriptions are concerned primarily with experiences of fear and the relationship to death. Only in them does the meaning of being manifest itself. Some, among them Bollnow and Binswanger, have therefore reproached Heidegger with having too narrow a basis. Other experiences for instance, experiences of happiness, also are ontologically relevant. But even if this be true, the fact remains that existential analytics will never constitute a comprehensive anthropology. The ontological viewpoint from the start requires a selection from the total complexity of the human.

Although he himself occasionally speaks of "existential anthropology," Heidegger therefore also delimits existentialism from anthropology—though he uses completely different arguments than Jaspers.[3] Anthropology sees in man only one realm of being among others. As with all beings it studies the being, man, in his particularity and special laws. But in so doing, it neglects the question of the being of this—and of all—being. This is the question existentialism poses. Existentialism does not want merely—to use an expression coined for another context—to be a "regional ontology," but a fundamental ontology. For it, man is, as it were, only the transparent place through which it looks at all being. Its starting point is man, but that is, so to speak, for lack of anything better. Existentialism would prefer to leap directly into being itself, and it spends time studying man only because he opens access to being for it. In Heidegger's later development the emphasis then shifts toward the pure question of being, while the existential analytics recedes completely into the background.

But as Heidegger's ontological objective limits anthropology, so vice versa: the starting point with man also limits ontological vision. Being does not come so multiperspectively into view as in real ontology. Thus for Heidegger anthropology and ontology interfere with one another, screen each other off. Like two trees that sprout from a single root, they rob each other of sap and light. The interlocking of the question of being and the question of man is what brought Heidegger fame, but it is sterile. We must, in the interest of both questions, release them both from this interlocking.

Anthropology and Marxism

As existentialism opposes anthropology despite a certain affinity with it, so Marxism has an analogous ambivalence. Marxism's first objection to philosophical anthropology is that the latter separates man from the historical process. It still believes in a supratemporal, fixed essence of man—just as ontology believes in the immutability of being—and it therefore deals with man as something that *is*, while in reality he is in a constant state of *becoming*. This objection can suggest two things. Either it means that anthropology admits of no philosophy of history that sets a predetermined highest final goal of man. In this sense the objection applies, but the answer is that precisely such a philosophy of history contains a fixed image of man. For though it teaches that mankind changes as it moves toward a far-off destination, still upon reaching it mankind would merely realize its true "nature," which was hovering before it from the first as an immutable and fixed ideal. Only the renunciation of such a philosophy of history permits the historicity of man to be seen as an unpreestablished, infinitely open adaptability. For only then is man no longer bound by a line of duty imposed from the outside, but he is himself the ultimate source of history, which he can freely shape. If the objection, in another sense, denies this insight, then it is simply false and stems from lack of knowledge about modern philosophical anthropology. For anthropology no longer identifies with any particular image, fixed in content, of man. When it speaks of a supratemporal nature of man, it is referring only to his formal structure—in fact, the inner openness by which man in the course of history undergoes change again and again. Anthropology, far from ignoring variability, supports it by revealing the conditions that cause it. Its relationship to human variability is like that of structural linguistics to the variety of languages.

Marxism's second objection claims that anthropology separates man from social reality, which conditions him down to his innermost core, and it is therefore really a form of "anthropologism," and, like Descartes, achieves only a "pseudo concreteness" (Kosik). But this objection also misses the mark, for where could man be more clearly placed within his social dimension than in Portmann, or in the cultural anthropology of Rothacker and Gehlen? The objection does apply fully to existentialism, which perhaps is the intended target rather than anthropology. Günther Anders first accused Heidegger of pseudo concreteness.

Since the discovery of Marx's "Paris manuscripts," which coincided in time with the rise of philosophical anthropology, there has existed, alongside official historical materialism, which eliminates the active subject in favor of objective, immanent social structures and historical processes, an anthropological interpretation of Marx, which seeks to "regain man's place in Marxism" (Sartre, opposed by Althusser). Herbert Marcuse has made a beginning: the young Marx's critique of capitalism is not based on economics but on an ideal picture of a meaningful, free realization of all essential human energies. This cannot succeed in the money- and product-oriented system of private property, which is hostile to man, severing him from the full reality of his existence and denaturing him into an alienated nonentity. As soon as man is made the true object of the national economy, which has never yet happened, the revolutionary demand for the abolition of private ownership of the means of production, along with the resulting alienation of labor and man's domination over man, follows logically. Only then is class society changed into human society. Man emerges from prehistory and his real history begins; indeed, as Engels agreed, he leaves the animal kingdom once and for all by overcoming the natural "struggle for individual existence."

At first Marx expected from this future state only the regaining of original human nature which had been lost during the interval of alienation. As early as 1845–1846, however, he abandoned this linear teleological model of history, in which history from the first was aiming for a particular goal and would be completed once that goal was reached (one could say: Marx turned from Hegel back to Herder). History, he now held, does not develop and realize a destiny of man that was fixed from the first; it is, rather, a process open to contingency, in which man acquires ever-new needs and exercises new activities, depending on the changing natural and social environment. Classless society is not a final state, but precisely with it "the development of new creative capacities, . . . the development of all human energies as such, . . . becomes a purpose in itself." Man produces his totality, he is contained completely within the process of becoming (*Das Kapital*).

Thus Marx joins the ranks of those who, starting with Herder, developed the line of study that is now called cultural and historical anthropology. Man is no longer, as he was for the Greeks, the theoretician who, himself just the reproduction of an eternal ideal, contemplates similar ideals, but the being who by his work creates his own world and himself within it—a suitable ideology for a bourgeois, industrial society. And this creation of himself and his world by man occurs not only once but again and again in an infinite unpredetermined historical process. That is Marx's Fichtean heritage, which he passed on to Sartre. Not only industry is "the open book of essential human energies," but so also are the forms of society, as well as art and science. Therefore man is, for Marx—despite his sixth thesis on Feuerbach—more than the "totality of social conditions, of the world-historical process." Though employed by production and group interests, the mind still preserves an autonomy by which it rises to the "realm of freedom." It is not the impersonal pseudo subjects but the mind that is the true subject of history. The mind itself has made, and can change, the conditions that determine it.

Stalinism had regarded the individual as a fellow fighter for the construction of socialism, with primary orientation toward collective plan fulfillment. Individuality and spontaneous activity therefore remained unemphasized in the philosophy of historical materialism, with its focus on the universal laws governing the evolution of society. Only after the end of the Stalinist era was it discovered that Marx was interested in a broad harmonious development of the individual. On the pattern of K. Korsch, a "Marxian humanism" developed; representative of this movement were: in Poland, Kolakowski and A. Schaff's *Philosophie des Menschen* ("Philosophy of Man"); the Yugoslavian *Praxis* group (Kangrga, Korac, Vranicki, Petrovic); and the Czechs, Kosik and Milan Machovez. All of them object to the reduction of man to his social and economic functions: man is richer, he is a center to himself. His freedom consists not only of "insight into necessity"; by creative initiative he must give new direction to the whole society and to his individual fate. Man's inner life is rediscovered; he must ask about the meaning of his action, has a claim on happiness, may in turn make claims on society. For this movement, "anthropology" is a stylish and vague word, perhaps even intentionally obscurant. What it really represents is a philosophy of freedom and the autonomous individual, and of personalism such as erupted elsewhere after repressive epochs, for instance in the Renaissance or in the Storm and Stress. But it is not only some political systems that today menace the individual and try to reduce him to a calculated factor within a vast manipulation; the danger is inherent in technological civilization as such. The call to leave room for man's independent decision and unviolated dignity is heard over the entire planet.

Part 2

MAN AND GOD
(Religious Anthropology)

CHAPTER 4

Anthropological Content of the Old and New Testaments

One of Scheler's anthropological projects which he never carried out was to write a history of the self-awareness of mankind, a history of the basic modalities of how man saw his position among the orders of being. He could present just an outline of this plan in his lecture "Man and History," and there he distinguished between five basic types of anthropology.

One of these basic types is religious anthropology. The oldest information about man is contained in the religious. Every faith reports not only of the nature and activity of the gods but also always something about man. Above all, his origin, the fate after death of his soul (which concept genuinely stems from religion), its damnation or salvation, are the domain of ancient religious lore. But also the tasks he has to fulfill in his life as a man and whose fulfillment gives meaning to his life are prescribed to early man by a religiously steeped tradition.

Human self-reflection first develops by confrontation with the gods. Homer calls the gods "the immortals," compared with whom man is "the mortal creature of a day," "the dream of a shadow" (Pindar, *Pythia* 8; cf. Ps. 62:9 and Ps. 116:11). Compared with the inhabitants of heaven man is *homo* (etymology *humus,* the one attached to the earth), compared with their lack of destiny he is a passive sufferer "cast by the water from cliff to cliff" (Hölderlin). By the superior power of the gods he becomes aware of his weakness, by their mysterious hiddenness he realizes the limitation of his knowledge. That he ought not to become arrogant, ought not in presumptuous hubris to seek to become like the gods, is a first principle of religious ethics. Yet he is not only compelled to bow before them; he may proudly feel related to them and chosen by them. "The race of men is one, the race of the gods another, but we all breathe from one breast" (Pindar, *Nemea* 6).

Already in antiquity the attempt was made to define man as the only being with religion. It was an idea that Berdyaev always repeated, "that the ontological question of man and the question of religion lie in the same stratum of existence." If with Rudolf Otto we accept the distinction between *mysterium tremendum* and *mysterium fascinosum,* then we do have to concede that the *mysterium tremendum* is not experienced exclusively by man. Animals too can experience an almost Acheronian horror before an unusual threat. But the animals seem to be debarred from *mysterium fascinosum,* an attraction by the eerie. Yet there is much else besides religion that is an exclusive property of man.

The Biblical Creation Account
as an Anthropological Document

The first chapters of Genesis amalgamate old anthropological myths. One such is already contained in the fact that Adam —this is actually not a proper name but means simply "the man" [1]—is said to be created by God. That is not so in all mythologies. Here man must not only honor God as the higher and stronger being, but he must also feel that he is his creature. At the same time this later provided a point of departure for the idea of his being a child of God.

More precisely, God creates man by creating a first couple from whom all men are then descended. Later this view of a common ancestry of mankind was called the monophyletic theory; the opposite theory is the polyphyletic. In the eighteenth century the monophyletists were the reactionary Biblical fundamentalists, the polyphyletists on the other hand were of the enlightened, progressive school.[2] But the modern theory of man's ancestry would seem to support the monophyletists. Of course the Bible has no intention of setting up a scientific thesis. Its primeval couple symbolizes man. It would be easier to draw an ethical thesis from the Biblical account; at least one has often been read into it later: that by our common descent from Adam we are all, including enemy nations, related to one another, that mankind constitutes one single large family.

Man communicates his creation by God to all the rest of "creation." But in the Bible the creation of the world is only a preparation for the creation of man. God does not create him together with the animals, but on his own day of creation: man originates from a new act of creation, he is—something which shocked later natural science—not a part of the animal kingdom, but a separate kingdom all by himself. And indeed God creates man on the last day of creation as the last living creature (according to modern biology, too, man appears as one of the last species on earth): man is the goal or at least the "crown of creation."

This is confirmed by the most important anthropological thesis of the creation account: "God made man in his image; in the image of God he made him." The other beings are only God's creatures; man, however, is his likeness, *imago dei*. Words full of implications, full of destiny, repeated thousands of times and later often used as postulates: man gains his highest dimension by virtue of his likeness to God: "You shall be holy, for I the Lord your God am holy" (Lev. 19:2; cf. Matt. 5:48).

There is also similarity between Homer's gods and men. But Homer's gods are "heightened men." Man's similarity to god here implies no problem. The Biblical statement, however, carries all the more weight because the Biblical God is tran-

scendent and incomprehensible. One not only should not make
an image of him, one cannot do so. How is it then possible
that man nonetheless is a likeness of him whom no image can
render? The contradiction can be explained if the creation
account contains an older stage in which God was still pictured anthropomorphically. What anthropomorphism in reality
is—the picturing of God according to the image of man—is
interpreted in reverse as the creation of man in the image of
God. The formless, purely spiritual God represents only a
later stage. From this later stage the attempt was then made
to interpret the statement of Genesis in the sense, for instance,
that the resemblance to God in man is his soul, his reason, or
his justice.[3]

Genesis itself also seems to find a resemblance to God in
men because they "rule over the fish of the sea, the birds
under the sky and the animals of the earth." Man represents
not merely a higher stage alongside the animals, he is also
their ruler.

The further human property that only man has speech as
opposed to the animals, though not expressly emphasized by
Genesis as a point of comparison between him and God, is
implicitly presented as such, for God produced the world by
speaking. But man did not receive language as a gift of God,
as later philosophy often teaches, but he himself "gives names."
He gives them especially "to all cattle, and to the birds of
the air, and to every beast of the field." This is probably meant
to underscore that this ability elevates him above them. (Similarly the Greeks actually call the animals *aloga,* i.e., nonrational and speechless.) Thus, as early as this, man is what
Herder called him, the "creature with language."

Despite man's likeness to God, however, the Bible never
leaves any doubt as to the tremendous distance between God
and man; indeed the Bible regards as the basic situation of
man the fact that he is situated at this distance, and that the
awareness of this can therefore never be sufficiently kept alive
and intensified. Perhaps the verse on man's likeness to God

should even be translated: God created man as his shadow image and only as a dark outline of himself. The second concept is meant to weaken the first still further. Never would the Bible celebrate man, as Homer does Telemachus, as "godlike"; never could its heroes, as in Greek mythology, boast of divine ancestry, or like Hercules be declared Gods after their death. Jews and Christians later came into real conflict with the Roman Empire because they could not go along with the cult of the emperor, which had been adopted from the Greeks. The Romans did not see that they wanted to be absolutely loyal—to "render to Caesar the things that are Caesar's"— and that only their totally different concept of God and man prevented them from paying religious homage to a living man. To be sure, for Christianity the Logos became flesh: God had assumed human form. And unending theological speculations are connected with this—e.g., *Cur deus homo?* (Anselm). The transcendent God takes on a human destiny in his Son. But this neither drags him down to the level of man nor lifts humanity to the divine.

How little the likeness to God draws man to God's level is shown in the prohibition against eating of the tree of knowledge.[4] God has reserved knowledge of good and evil for himself. That knowledge of good and evil is a divine property and will make man like to God is what the serpent says in its words of seduction.

Giving in to its temptation, Adam and Eve eat of the tree of knowledge. In this way they arrogate to themselves a divine quality that God did not intend for them: man is an ethical being, knowing good and evil, and precisely this is a divine trait in him. He has seized it from God against God's intention. He wins his highest quality through guilt. Little as he resembles the Titans in their rivalry with God, still Prometheus comes to mind, for he had to steal fire for men from the gods. And as he is punished for his guilt, so are Adam and Eve: they are expelled from Paradise.[5]

And that does not mean merely that they have to exchange

the beautiful garden for the rough field. Beside the tree of
knowledge there grew in Paradise the tree of eternal life.
Originally Adam and Eve had been permitted to eat of it:
it was not at all prohibited. But after they have committed
sacrilege, God takes back the godlike immortality he had
originally intended for them. He had announced this punishment from the first in case of their violation. "From the day
on which you eat of it you will be mortal." He casts them
out of Paradise and places an angel before it "to guard the
path to the tree of life," from which they thus remain forever
separated. This means: man must die; and he is himself to
blame for this fate.

In connection with this later so-called "fall into (original)
sin" the Biblical author brings together a whole series of
further human properties he has observed. He has already
noted that man, as distinguished from the beasts, has a sense
of shame and wears clothes, that he is the only creature that
must work to earn a living, and that the human female suffers
more strongly from pregnancy ailments and birth pains. Now
all this must be mythically explained and a cause for it be
given. Originally, so it says, Adam and Eve went naked "and
were not ashamed"; only by eating of the tree of knowledge
were "their eyes opened" to this (but that doesn't mean that
good and evil originally had to do only with the area of sexuality). Originally man did not have to work; in Paradise he
got his food without effort. That he now must work, and also
woman's pains at childbirth, both these things—as well as
mortality—are now interpreted as a divine penalty for vio-
lating God's prohibition, as a curse to an existence that is so
hard only for that reason.

Already in Genesis two opposite valuations of man clash
together, one that elevates him and one that debases him, and
they result perhaps necessarily from the ambivalence of the
basic religious feeling, in which being uplifted by God and
destroyed by him are juxtaposed in "contrast harmony" (R.

Otto). (The polarity of national pride and admiration for foreign countries are probably a corollary to this.) The world as a whole, too, is close to God from one perspective because created by him: he wanted and ordained it so. But at the same time there is an abyss between God and the world: he remains its ruler; he is holy, and it is not. Compared with the rest of creation, man's nearness to God is much greater: God has chosen him as his likeness. But compared with God he too shares the nondivinity of every created thing, he has sinned against God and been punished by him. Thus man's self-awareness here is strangely divided. The feeling of being elevated yet dependent, pride, and humility mingle in it. Psalm 8 also juxtaposes the two aspects: "What is man that thou art mindful of him?" and yet, "Thou dost crown him with glory and honor." Here Pascal's words add: "When he glorifies himself, I humiliate him; when he humbles himself, I glorify him," and: "Man infinitely surpasses man." [6]

Man the Sinner

In the Old Testament, Adam and Eve sinned, and therefore men no longer live in Paradise, but this does not at all mean that everyone born thereafter shares this guilt. To this day the pious Jew does not live in the feeling of being burdened with an original sin. The fall of the first man did not corrupt all human nature. "The soul that you have laid in me, it is pure."

In contrast, extreme forms of Christian theology understand man as *homo peccator* (man the sinner). He is imperfect and worthless, not only as compared to God; he is also fundamentally sinful and guilty as such. He lives constitutionally in a state of deficiency.

And yet sinfulness is not insurmountable. God's grace can redeem from it. Sinfulness is therefore both a need of redemption and a capacity for it. But only faith can make one worthy of redemption. Therefore faith seems to be the only original act appropriate to man.

Sinfulness must however be understood not in a moral but in a purely religious or, if one wishes, metaphysical sense. Just like anyone else, even a person of high morals participates, by the very fact of being a man, in the general sinfulness. The guilt in which we stand implicated before God, does not stem from individually committed violations. Therefore it cannot be avoided or repaired through one's own merit, but only grace can lift one out of it. One's own merit is not even a step toward grace; in fact, it is often an impediment. For precisely the person who is obedient to the law and morally strict easily inclines to self-righteousness and so, despite all moral goodness, fails to become aware of his need for redemption, which continues nevertheless; thereby he is even doubly condemned: "He perceives nothing of God's spirit." But the morally lost person is by that very fact inclined to recognize himself humbly in his extramoral lostness. "The tax collectors [i.e., cheats] and the harlots go into the kingdom of God before you [i.e., the Pharisees]." And Paul says quite similarly (I Cor. 1:26 f.): "Not many . . . of noble birth" are called, but God has chosen what is "ignoble and despised in the eyes of the world and what is nothing to destroy what is something, so that no flesh may pride itself before him." (Therefore he also proclaims to the slave: you are the master and your master is the slave!) Earthly and divine standards, the ethical and the religious go separate ways.

There is a dilemma in the fact that man is said to be rotten and sinful yet created by God who is almighty, good, and merciful. In this dilemma the legend of the fall into sin gains a new function. As man came forth out of the hand of God, in his "original state in Paradise," he was still perfect. Only by disobeying God's prohibition, that is, by his own guilt, did he end up in his present ruin. God—who had equipped him with the ability to resist it—cannot be reproached for it.

But the individual human likewise cannot be reproached for it. That is just the difference from moral guilt, which he can be blamed for. Each individual finds himself already sinful as a member of the human race; he is sinful only because of original sin, which Adam as the first man brought down upon all men and which is communicated from generation to generation. By the very fact that we exist after the Fall we all share in original sin. Sinfulness is therefore for us post-Adamites an original inheritance of human nature. Adam's fall has vitiated our nature.

But precisely the fact that our nature was not always sinful contains a truth of infinite depth. First of all, the concept of an original condition prior to sin follows directly from the structure of etiological myth, which explains what is in terms of its origin and therefore necessarily presupposes a (timeless) prior state. Men are sinful, says the myth, because the first man sinned: therefore he must once have been sinless. But it also follows that sin is not the true and ultimate nature of man. Hidden behind it is a more genuine and higher nature. And this supplies the deepest reason why he can long for and hope to obtain redemption. Therefore redemption, though only God can grant it, is virtually already inherent in him. It brings him nothing fundamentally new but only gives him back what he once had and lost.

But just as there is more joy in heaven over one penitent sinner than over a thousand just men, the state of grace that is given back differs from the one he once lost. It does re-create the original one but it does this on a higher turn of the spiral, or as Hegel would put it, on a dialectically higher level (Hegel actually drew inspiration for his dialectics from this cross section of salvation history). Therefore Augustine could exclaim: *"Felix culpa!"* ("O happy guilt!") For Adam's sin was the precondition for redemption and therefore for a higher salvation than mankind would have obtained had it remained in the state of Paradise. (Similar logic produced the medieval Judas sects, which honored the very betrayer of

Christ because without him Christ would not have died for us on the cross. Through his moral guilt he became metaphysically an instrument of grace and is therefore justified after the fact.)

Like the Fall, redemption is an event in time; it appears in and with Christ. Of course, even after Christ's coming each individual has to assure himself of redemption through faith and the sacraments, by being awakened by Christ and reborn in him. Yet in a deeper sense mankind as a whole is already redeemed by the appearance of Christ as such. By taking on himself the sins of mankind he opened a new era of grace. Adam and Christ are thus the two cornerstones of human history. The direct protection of grace which Adam lost by his betrayal has been restored by Christ. After long centuries of defection, mankind returns to God's bosom. As was seen above, contrary to all purely philosophical anthropology, which seeks to investigate a constant nature of man, a new insight is gained: man is a historical being and undergoes deep transformations in the course of his history; he is different depending on his place in time. Adam before and after the fall, mankind before and after Christ, is in each case different not only peripherally but down to his deepest essence. Anthropology reaches its culmination in a philosophy of history.

The Anthropology of the Apostle Paul

Paul distinguishes between two groups of men: those who live according to the flesh and those who live according to the spirit. (Here Paul probably is recalling that God blew his breath, his spirit, into the first man.) There are natural and spiritual men, the unconverted and the converted, the lost and the saved, children of the world and children of God. The first group is derived from Adam, the second from Christ.

The "natural man" is not, however, as one might perhaps believe at first sight, a coarse primitive! Paul is not concerned with secular differences such as culture and good breeding. The opposite of natural man is not the cultured man, but the one who has received grace. The natural man may well be philosophically educated and guided by ethical principles. One often has the impression that Paul draws his picture of the natural man practically from the Greek philosophers. In this, Paul manifests a trait of character of all noble minds, in principle not to debase one's enemy but to see him in his highest possibility. But all such thoroughly respectable wisdom of natural man is, after all, only "human wisdom," "wisdom of this world," not the "hidden wisdom of God." Natural man proudly sees being a man as a supreme value. To him the Spirit of God is a folly he absolutely refuses to accept. And therefore, despite his excellent qualities, he remains stuck in sin.

On the contrary, the spiritual man may be ignorant and sinful, but nonetheless the Spirit of God, by which he is deeply moved and on which he knows he depends, makes him a child of God. As a temple of God in which the Spirit of God dwells (I Cor. 3:16) he stands above the merely fleshly and natural man. "Now we have received not the spirit of the world, but the Spirit which is from God"; we "speak not with words which human wisdom can teach, but with words which the holy Spirit teaches" (I Cor. 2:12 f.).

But the spiritual man too is not born as such but is transformed from the fleshly man.

Similarly in the Greek mysteries the process of becoming man took place in two phases: the primeval men were unfinished and lacked organized human form even externally.[7] Only through the divinity which brought culture did they enter into the second and final phase of being men. This process of full humanization was what the mysteries celebrated anew. Therefore the mystic elite felt that they were the only true men as opposed to the uninitiated. They called themselves teleioi, i.e., the perfected. Similarly within Christianity, Tatian teaches that man as a rational creature is still not truly man, only the one "who has progressed beyond his humanity to God" becomes truly a man.

As is already presupposed in the Old Testament concept of *teshuba,* according to Paul a sudden conversion, a transforming rebirth, must take place. Still an opponent and persecutor of Christians in his youth, Paul himself experienced such a sudden rebirth on the way to Damascus. God makes us blessed "through the bath of rebirth and renewal of the Holy Spirit" (Titus 3:5; cf. Rom. 12:2; 6:4 and 7:6). The spiritual man who has taken off the old and "put on" the new man (Eph. 4:22-24, cf. Col. 3:9,10) is another, new man, a "new foundation" (II Cor. 5:17). But however much man may long for such a spiritual renewal, he can never bring it about himself. It remains a gift of God.

That there are experiences with which "another life" (Plotinus) begins for men is a tradition of all mysticism, and is also evidence that contact with God and the breakthrough of a new man out of the old resulting from it can take place only in a sudden "leap" (*raptus*). This is countered by other experiences according to which the new factor in man grows only gradually and gains ascendancy not by revolution but by evolution. In still other experiences it never really gains a complete victory: we can only struggle toward it. Thus according to Augustine, man who was made ill by the fall into sin struggles in vain here on earth to regain health without ever reaching it: "As long as we live, we struggle." "For I was a man, and that means to struggle." What we are left with is ultimately only desire and striving, and only "on the sabbath of eternal life will we rest in you." These three experiences, however, correspond to three types of men, each disposed to one or another of them.

Even after the divine pneuma has entered the natural man, however, the natural part in him continues to exist. The spiritual man is divided into a double nature: flesh and spirit, Adam and Christ. Paul sometimes calls these two men who are in us the "external" and the "inner" man (II Cor. 4:16, cf. Rom. 7:22). In another passage (II Cor. 4:7) he distinguishes between the earthly vessel that man is by nature alone —an old and still living metaphor—and the glorious treasure which God's action through Christ laid into this vessel. The flesh becomes the "temple of the Holy Spirit" (I Cor. 6:19).

This division of man into an external vessel and an internal hidden treasure seems to recall the Orphic doctrine (which goes back to still older religious lore) of the body (sōma) as a mere "mark" (sēma) of the soul, as Plato in his *Phaedo* has impressively described it for all time. Paul himself—who had knowledge at least of the Hellenistic popular philosophy— gives some ground for the confusion of his distinction with the Platonic one by sometimes speaking of the spirit living in man also as his inner life, his awareness (of being a child of God) and his soul. But for Paul this means something completely different.

According to Plato, evil stems only from the body; the soul is the pure, divine principle in us. It still remains so even after Plato had to admit that some evil is inborn even in the soul. For Paul, however, natural man as a whole is sinful, and even his soul is not excepted from this as his unaffected better part. There is no opposition of the bad body and the good soul, but the soul too—which in Paul often sounds like a translation of the Old Testament "life" [8]—belongs completely on the side of the earthly (similarly to the language of the Greek mysteries). Therefore Paul interchangeably calls natural man "fleshly" or "natural." Body and soul have their common counterpart in the spirit. Therefore whoever is schooled in Plato's thinking has to rethink completely. Others have later sought to bring the Platonic and the Pauline conceptions into harmony with one another and thus arrived at a tripartition. Justin calls the body a house of the soul, the soul a house of the spirit. For this reason Clement and Origen distinguished three types of men depending on their predominant component: hylic, psychic, and pneumatic.

But really Paul's anthropology—though some of his statements invite misunderstanding—is not at all dualistic. He does not replace the Platonic soul with the spirit and contrast it with both body and soul as Plato opposed soul to body. For Paul the spiritual man as a whole, including his body, is spiritual. Die and become! In the bath of transformation everything in him is integrated into the cleansing spirit. Therefore Christianity also knows not only the immortality of the soul but also a (cf. I Cor., ch. 15) "resurrection of the flesh" (a concept which at that time provoked the mockery of pagan philosophy at the crowding which this would cause in heaven). This is an extraordinary reversal of our usual idea of the Greeks and Christianity: the Greeks, who are considered pagan affirmers of the body, are the dualists. Plato places the soul over against the body and only the soul becomes immortal. While Christianity, to which hostility to the body and the stressing of pure interiority are generally attributed, is originally (as is Jewish culture) opposed to any body-soul dualism and therefore has the body, too, participate in glory beyond the grave.

CHAPTER 5

Five Main Theses of Religious Anthropology and Their Rebuttal

Theocentricity

In the Bible, God creates man. He creates him in his image. The antithesis of this is: man is the one who creates God. And man too makes God in his own image. Man is not a shadow image of God, but God is an idealized image of man. "In his gods man depicts himself" (Schiller). We have already mentioned Xenophanes' attack on the anthropomorphism of the Homeric gods. But Xenophanes was no atheist. He is the first one who formulated a new, philosophical concept of God. Later, numerous theories on the origin of religion arose which rationalistically relegated the divine completely to the role of a human product.

Euhemerus, who was associated with the Epicureans, wrote a novel, *Hiera Anagraphē*, in which he narrated that on an island in the ocean he had found an inscription describing the heroic deeds of Cronus and Zeus. Obviously therefore they had been only mighty monarchs of vanished kingdoms and had been deified only subsequently—like the contemporary Hellenic rulers. In this manner Euhemerus wanted to reduce the gods to men, great figures of the historic past.

In the Western world the Renaissance and the Enlightenment awakened a new self-consciousness in men, which rebelled against any dependence. Exhilarated by his own creative powers and knowledge, man wants to rely only on himself. He no longer wants to be a member of God's kingdom, but wants to feel that he is master of his own domain of life. Feuerbach, as already mentioned, reduced God most crudely to a projection of man. Just as for Hegel the world spirit attains consciousness only by way of its own historical manifestations, so for Feuerbach the human spirit becomes aware of itself, not by direct reflection and turning back upon itself but only by projecting itself outward. Only in objectified form can it get a view of itself. And as Hegel's divine spirit objectifies itself in human history, so Feuerbach's human spirit objectifies itself in God. God is merely the externalized and objectified "image of man given autonomy by his imagination." God's omnipotence corresponds to the omnipotence of the human spirit; God's justice, to our moral sense; God's goodness, to our own temperament. In God we therefore sum up our own self. "Man's knowledge of God is man's knowledge of himself."

Both Hegel and Feuerbach are dependent on Kant for this conviction that the spirit knows itself only from its own projections, as one sees oneself in a mirror. According to Kant, we arrive at the categories of our thought only by asking back from the fact of the sciences in which these categories have materialized transcendentally to the conditions of their possibility. Kant's epistemological method is extended by Hegel and Feuerbach to metaphysics and cultural history. Later Dilthey gave it an individual, psychological turn: one's own self-knowledge too is gained not by introspection but by way of its earlier "expression."

After he has unmasked God as a mere projection, Feuerbach strives to transfer back to man the qualities that had been lent to God. Since all statements about God from the first were statements about man, one needs only to discover the true meaning of these statements by reversing them and interchanging subject and predicate. If Christianity says, "God suffers for others," then the true transposition is: "Suffering for others is divine." In this manner, step by step, God is deprived of existence and his entire richness is heaped upon man. Theology, which always was only anthropology in disguise, dissolves into a manifest anthropology. "God was my first thought, reason my second, man my third and last thought."

Feuerbach was blind to real religion. But his construction of a critique of religion is appealing because its main accent is set not so much on the dethronement of God as on the elevation of man. If earlier thinkers resisted the human form of God with the argument that God was nobler than everything human, Feuerbach does the opposite and considers man the noblest and believes that God derives his nobility only from man. Feuerbach is an opponent of religion only because it is an obstacle to man's true estimation of himself and robs him of his greatness and glory. These must be stolen from the imaginary realm and given back to real man. Man must learn to cease hoping futilely for his wishes to be fulfilled in the beyond, and must realize them by his own actions in this world. Man, once he is freed from God, not only will have a higher concept of himself but will rise higher in reality (later Marx held the same belief). Feuerbach's antitheism turns out to be prohominism. The attack on God serves as a defense of man.

Similarly Nietzsche[1] says (and Sartre again took up this idea): "God is dead" (this was a literal quotation from Bruno Bauer); "now we want the superman to live" (*Thus Spoke Zarathustra*, IV). Nietzsche too intended man to take over God's inheritance; indeed, God has so hindered man's full development that only his downfall clears the way for the ultimate and highest possibility of man, the superman. Nietzsche was convinced that we are living in the hour of human history that he called "the great midday" when the death of God and the birth of the superman are taking place. Here too it is the mortal god who is rebelling against the immortal one.

From an ethical perspective Max Scheler and Nicolai Hartmann arrived at a "postulatory atheism" (Scheler). For Kant, God (theoretically undemonstrable) was still a postulate of practical reason as a protector of the moral order of the world, so that the good might find happiness after death. But Hartmann, at the conclusion of his *Ethik* (cf. also his posthumous work *Teleologisches Denken*, "Teleological Thinking"), lists five irresoluble antinomies between religion and morality. Religion, he says, destroys man as a moral person. Especially the existence of the world ruler who independently helps the good man to victory would rob man of all responsibility and take away from him his personal task of endowing the world with meaning.

Anthropocentricity

Just as the religious world view makes God the lord of the world, it makes man master of the earth under God's special care. The religious world view is not only theocentric, it is also anthropocentric. This does not constitute a contradiction. And therefore it is also not contradictory when modern thought, rejecting theocentricity, underscores man's independence, yet at the same time opposes anthropocentricity.

Already in the Old Testament loud opposition was raised to man's placing himself in the center. When Job (chs. 38 ff.) demands that God treat him with special protection, he is instructed that God created not only man but everything in the world. No creature has a higher claim on him than any other.

The most permanent undermining of human presumption to assume a privileged place in the world came from Copernicus. As long as men believed in the Ptolemaic theory that the earth was the center of the universe, it was feasible to ascribe this central position to man also. But now that the earth has become only "a star among the stars," belief in the exceptional singularity of man is also untenable. As Nicholas of Cusa had reflected, on other planets there may live creatures equal to us or even higher. The church was quick to recognize the anthropological consequence of the Copernican theory. It considered the theory more than a strictly astronomical error; it rightly feared that this theory would bring about a complete change of the former sense of life and the world. This is the real reason for the bitterness with which the church attacked this theory. Copernicus himself had dedicated his work to the pope and he died without facing any hostility; but the church waged a persistent inquisitorial struggle against Galileo and Giordano Bruno because of Copernicus. Bruno was burned for his convictions in 1600—less than four hundred years ago!

But it was precisely Giordano Bruno who transformed Copernicanism and blunted its edge. Copernicus had replaced the geocentric system with a heliocentric one. The earth and man with it were now relegated to an arbitrary peripheral point in the universe. Bruno, however, represents the Renaissance's experience of infinity. Unlike antiquity and the Middle Ages, the Renaissance no longer considers the world to be finite. But where there is no limit, there is also no center. Or one can just as easily say: the center is everywhere. Cusa knew this; as an old mystical formula expressed it: "God is a sphere whose center is everywhere (circumference nowhere)." But in that case Copernicus is doubly wrong: the sun cannot replace the earth as the center, for there is no longer a center; but then the earth remains unchangedly the center, for the center is everywhere.

Bruno goes even farther. For the Middle Ages the earth was indeed the center, but the impure, terrestrial (sublunar) sphere was sharply distinguished from the purer, lunar one and this again, from the purest, the solar (or sidereal) sphere. Each of these spheres was considered to be of qualitatively different constitution, and a connection between them seemed impossible (therefore it was even denied that meteors fall from heaven). The Renaissance on the other hand, because of its pantheistic feeling, abandoned this separation of the spheres.

The world becomes at every point a divinely permeated cosmic reality. (Newton's much-admired discovery that one and
the same natural force, gravitation, both draws the apple to
the ground and spins the moon around the earth, that the same
mechanisms apply in the sky as on earth, and that there is
a "mechanics of the heavens"—this discovery could succeed
only in the context of this new feeling of the pervasive unity
of the world.) Bruno concludes from the new feeling of the
world's unity that the earthly sphere too is enveloped in the
glory that was formerly considered to be only sidereal. A new
star in the sky has been discovered: the earth. "We are already
in heaven" he rejoices—and this connotes for him: we no
longer need the church's heaven. Though Christian self-awareness had always been accompanied by humble submission to
God, in Bruno it is replaced by the self-confidence of the
Renaissance individual, who knows that in his autonomy and
creative power he himself is "another God." That is the reason
why the church persecuted Bruno: not because he flung man
out of the divine shelter into the lostness of infinite space,
but because he deified man himself; not because he undid
anthropocentrism but because he even overdid it.

In the eighteenth century the idea of man as the center of
the world gained a new acceptance, but in a narrow-minded
and exaggerated form. Leibniz had taught only that God had
given the world an intrinsically purposeful order; now Wolff
teaches: he ordained it to man's purpose. A similar degeneration of thought takes place in the transition from Aristotle
to the Stoics.[2] According to Wolff, the sun shines so that man
will not freeze and so that he can see; at night it goes down so
that he can sleep; at the same time the moon shines so that
we will not be left in complete darkness if we have to get up
at night! Man feels in the world like the guest at a spa hotel,
where everything is arranged to meet his needs. That was not
the Biblical view, nor did Nietzsche intend this later when he
called man the "meaning of the earth." Schiller, in a famous

distich, had lampooned the anthropistic self-conceit implicit in a teleological orientation of the world toward man, according to which the cork tree grows only so that man can put stoppers on his bottles. Likewise Goethe—though, in opposition to mechanism, he believed in final forces at work in nature—spoke out against an "anthropo-final" tendency of all nature. Therefore he praised Spinoza, whom he considered his comrade-in-arms on this issue, for his "boundless unselfishness"; this much-quoted phrase suggests that Spinoza too had recognized no orientation of nature toward man.

As Copernicus had done in astronomy, Darwin later in biology dealt a hard blow to faith in the priviliged position of man. According to the Bible, God created man in a special act of creation. But according to Darwinism, man, like all the other species, stems directly from the animal kingdom. No original chasm separates him and the animal kingdom. Just as man has developed historically, so he can one day perish. "Life on earth: a moment, an incident, an exception without result," says Nietzsche, and the species of animal called man also has its delimited life-span: "So many species of animals have already vanished." Thus even in this regard man is disrobed of his supposed singularity. Just as for Copernicus he inhabits just any point in the universe, so for Darwinism he constitutes just any point of transition in the general organic process of evolution. No longer the priests, but the zoologist has the last word about him.

Human self-awareness, it has been said, has undergone three shocks in the course of the last several centuries. The Copernican revolution and Darwinism are joined by historicism. As in the Biblical religions man believes himself chosen above all other creatures, so within the world of men each single group believes itself chosen above all the others, so that only its views, values, and mores are true, only it is the bearer of the culture that is truly fitting for mankind. This naïve conviction has since the end of the eighteenth century been brought into doubt by historicism: all forms of culture are in principle equal, one may measure none by the others and least of all someone else's by one's own. Through this view man's previously unbroken self-awareness also loses all basis and support. What he considered absolute turns out to be one experiment among others.

The Doctrine of Original Sin

The awareness of a guilt for which we have to "justify" ourselves before God has engraved itself so deeply into Western man that it still sets the tone even when its original religious origin has long been given up and forgotten. Man is made of "wood too crooked" for him ever to become completely straight, we read in the otherwise progressive Kant, who stems from a Pietistic family. Kant also spoke of the "radical evil" in man, whereby he, as Goethe said, spotted his philosophical robe. That something in man is broken, that he is deeply hurt and sick, that is the mood in which Nietzsche has his Zarathustra exclaim: "You have not suffered enough from man!" Certainly it is not Christian sinfulness under which he is suffering. And yet in a general sense, whoever loves man as enthusiastically as Nietzsche did suffers all the more deeply from him. Only in his new nature, which no longer would be man in the previous sense, in the superman, could the dormant nobler seed in man begin to develop. Existentialism also takes the same line of reasoning: it unrolls a dark view of life before us, a veritable kaleidoscope of "fallen" man with no likeness to God and with his disorientation, questionableness, and inadequacy, with his failure and his absurdity.

One of the first objections to be directed against the doctrine of sinfulness relates to a distortion of this teaching. For Paul, the fleshly man was the same as the natural man as contrasted with the spiritual. By this he did not mean the flesh in the literal sense, nor did he mean sexuality. But in and since Augustine, "flesh" often acquires the narrower meaning of "sexuality."

"The flesh is weak" still means only: man cannot resist his sexual desires. And sin is now equated with these desires. "Original sin" is interpreted quite unhistorically by Augustine as the succumbing to the sin of sex. Chastity then takes on the semblance of the highest virtue, from then all the way to Tolstoi. The "lust of the flesh" is supposedly justified only in marriage; some extreme movements even condemn it there. Asceticism, mortification of the flesh, and self-castigation become a preparation for redemption most pleasing to God. Thus the Christian West knows but little erotic culture. Eroticism, excluded from the sanctification of life, falls prey to the demonic.

Within Christianity, only the Renaissance, which reappropriated attitudes from antiquity, and Luther gave us back our good conscience toward sexuality. In his reverence for everything natural Goethe writes to Lavater that he finds the Christian dogmas of the Immaculate Conception and the Virgin Birth repulsive. This affirmation of the "natural" also continues in modern times (sports also, for example, have taken away our shame regarding the human body). Psychoanalysis has revealed the harmful effects of excessive sexual repression and established the formula: one ought to repress one third of the libido, sublimate one third, and live one third. The call for asceticism is probably the aspect of Christianity whose meaning is least understood today. We are awakening from a thousand-year nightmare and finally beginning to breathe freely again.

The interpretation of original sin as sexual sin is, however, as we said, only a restrictively false interpretation. The idea of original sin has a broader meaning than that. Therefore its denial must be more broadly based. In the eighteenth century, fostered by pantheistic, world-affirming roots, the opposite idea of the original goodness of man and the resuscitation of pre-Christian and non-Christian pride in this world gained acceptance, with very real results, e.g., for pedagogy. As long as it was assumed that man is evil by nature, a punitive type of pedagogy aimed at restraining and deterring evil prevailed—in line with Luther's idea that the old Adam had to be drowned every day and Hobbes's idea that natural egoism can be broken only by coercion. If man is, on the other hand, by nature good, as Locke and Rousseau affirmed, then it is enough to let his good dispositions grow and lovingly encourage their development. Later Nietzsche soared beyond these alternatives: life is neither good nor bad, but it stands beyond both—or, as could also be said, both are mixed in one Dionysian retort. With unspeakable severity he accuses Christianity—whose concept of guilt he understands in a purely moral and not in a metaphysical sense—of robbing human development of its innocence. Man is not sick by nature, Christianity is what has made him sick. Nietzsche's new religion of life is meant to restore man's good health.

A sort of synthesis between faith in the wickedness and perdition of man and faith in his goodness and perfection is represented by the theory of perfectibility and progress of the eighteenth and nineteenth centuries: though human affairs were in the past and are today in bad shape, we are gradually developing toward greater perfection. Man is therefore both good and bad—however, not simultaneously but successively: evil dominates the beginning of history, goodness gains ascendancy in the course of time.

And yet in this synthesis, goodness predominates. According to the theory of progress, even the man who is still imperfect has within himself the seeds of perfection: otherwise he could not set progress toward it in motion. That he has not yet reached perfection affects only his temporary historical appearance. Intrinsically his object in life is perfection, which he is asymptotically approaching. Thus the theory of progress proves to be the secularization of the Christian metaphysics of history. Man must be transformed and gradually purified from a state of sin to a state of grace, but this process only develops and intensifies his original goodness.

The same applies to the great opponent of the theory of progress, Rousseau. In fact, the analogy with the Christian scheme of salvation is even more evident in him. As in the Bible, man comes forth pure out of the hand of the Creator. As in the Bible, man brings about his own downfall. In Rousseau's theory the "fall into sin" consists precisely of so-called progress and civilization. And therefore Rousseau too has the desire for a return to the starting point in Paradise, a return to "nature" which can, he believes, be brought about by reversing so-called progress. Thus it seems as if the Christian three-stage anthropology—original state, state of sin, state of grace—recurs in Rousseau in secular garb.

And yet a closer look shows that the emphasis is distributed quite differently. For Christianity, the state of sin is the true reality of life. The original condition is only a remote memory, a metaphysical dream without efficacy for the present. And the state of grace, though Christ has already initiated it, still remains just a promise, both for the individual and for mankind as a whole. For Rousseau, however, civilization's state of sin is only something ephemeral, an intermediary condition that arose only in historical time and will be surmountable in the historically near future. The determining factor characteristic of man is not this temporary blight of civilization but his former natural perfection. And this gives him the inherent power to regain this earlier quality by his own insight and effort.

The Doctrine of Grace

The theory of progress opposes the Christian doctrine of sin by its faith in the original goodness of man, but it also is against the Christian doctrine of grace. For in Christianity, fallen man, powerless of himself, can be saved only by the gift of divine grace. The theory of progress, however, holds that man, whom it regards as not fallen very deep, can lift himself up by his own power and "work his way up the paths to Olympus." Both know a "self-redemption."

But Christianity itself has variously strict formulations of the doctrine of grace. It admits of no self-redemption, but still various Christian teachings allow for some participation on man's part in his salvation. The point at issue between Augustine and Pelagius was whether every human effort, however pure, is inadequate and vain and we can be saved only by grace—*sola gratia*—or whether man can move at least a bit toward grace and, as it were, prepare the ground for it. Pelagius too held that man's salvation does not depend totally on himself but needs a supernatural completion. But for him an innate nobility dwells in us. Because of this innate natural nobility we are not completely dependent on an outpouring of salvation from above, but can strive toward it on our own. God's efficacy and his activity in man are joined by human cooperation.

Augustine, on the contrary, regards sinfulness as a basic property of man, which has been imposed on man by God, and which we cannot change by our own power, for only God by his grace can remove it. Whether we perform good works or not, they do not contribute to the obtaining of grace. And so Augustine formulates statements almost weird in their religious radicalism: e.g., *"Ama deum et fac quod vis"* ("Love God and do what you will!").

This sentence is often interpreted as though it meant: whoever truly loves God can do no evil; he needs no further guideline than to do the right thing on his own. Augustine means something quite different: the believer is still capable of committing evil; but for grace, so he believes, that is not important, it does not direct itself by good behavior or evil deed.

Augustine is thinking religiously while Pelagius, though not denying the religious significance of sin and that grace is a free gift, does not want to remove moral responsibility from our own shoulders. In Pelagius, as his opponents have correctly seen, there still lives a portion of "pagan" antiquity. Man is, for him, not exclusively dependent on divine mercy, but himself achieves something through his mind and will. Although Pelagianism was bitterly persecuted in its time, a modified form of it, called semi-Pelagianism, survived in Catholicism. Original sin has weakened the divine spark in man but not extinguished and destroyed it completely. By his actions man can earn merit through his "good works," and he can climb a few stages of knowledge of God in a "natural theology" prior to any revelation, relying on his own reason. Just as grace does not do away with morality, revelation does not devalue the truth of philosophy. It is not a coincidence that the above-mentioned Lafitau, who was the first to value the natural ethics and religiosity of the non-Christian peoples was a Jesuit Pelagian.

Luther, however, continues the line of Paul and Augustine. Original sin so harmed human nature that it is vitiated to the core and completely ruined in a perdition from which it cannot rise by its own power. Not by moral merit but by faith—*sola fide*—can we hope to participate in God's renewing grace. Not rational knowledge but only the revealed word of the Bible tells us anything about God. According to Luther—and Calvin, even more—man is completely sinful and weak, all darkness opposed to God's light. This is the difference between the Reformation and mysticism, though the subjective experience of faith is stronger in both than in previous ages. The mystic finds God in the depth of his own soul; for the Reformation he remains completely transcendental.

But Luther can be contrasted not only with Catholicism but also with humanism such as that of Erasmus, who in his famous polemical tract *On Free Will* upheld the inner freedom of man against Luther. And this humanistic faith that man can perform great things by his own power gradually gains ascendancy in the eighteenth century and especially in the genius cult and ideals of freedom in the Goethe period. "Did you not do everything yourself, sacredly ardent heart?"—such Promethean Titanism and defiance of God is one extreme on the scale.

The most radical denial of the doctrine of grace, however, is its reversal. God depends on man's good favor. According to an ancient doctrine native to Iran, the world is the scene of the struggle between a good and an evil principle. In this cosmic struggle man has to take sides; he ought to put himself on the side of the good principle and become an ally of God, indeed perhaps the ultimate victory of light over darkness depends on his decision and energy. Max Scheler even goes a step farther. He amalgamates this doctrine with the Gnostic idea that God is not statically perfect but in the process of becoming, and with the mystical idea that "without me God cannot for a moment live." Therefore according to Scheler, man is more than an ally of God. Rather, he is the one who makes God real by an unending "theogenetic" process. Man, by filling the world more and more with meaning, by converting more and more areas of his value system into reality, "weaves the living garment of God." Man's own activity, which formerly was nothing or counted but slightly compared with what God performs in us, now itself becomes the effecter of God.

Faith in Immortality

The Stoics held that our individual reason is only a mode and center of activity of one single cosmic reason. Therefore it demands the same thing everywhere and binds classes and nations. The world logos is identical with the logos that acts in each one of us. Our soul is not at all our property but only a splinter of the *"âme universelle unique,"* as Malebranche later says, like a spark of the eternal divine fire. Therefore it does not perish after our death, it continues to exist but—as especially Averroës expressed it—not really as ours but only in the universal soul. Similarly for the Hindus life after death does not consist in the preservation of one's individual, separate existence but in resubmergence into the preindividual foundation of being.

In Christianity as in many other religions and philosophies, however, a personal existence beyond the grave awaits each one of us. In life itself, after all, Christianity expects an individual relationship to God from each person and discovers, in

Harnack's words, "the infinite value of the individual soul." In this respect Christianity can rightly claim to be a precursor of the modern breakthrough, by Nicholas of Cusa, Leibniz, Schleiermacher, and others, to the appreciation of the individual, whether human or nonhuman. In contrast to Platonism, the highest value is seen as residing not in the general but in the unique singular object that is never repeated.

As we have seen, in Christianity the body also participates in life beyond the grave. Under the impression of the corruption of the body the idea soon emerged that not the whole man but only his soul becomes immortal. Originally that is what "soul" meant, namely, the quintessence of the numinous in us as contrasted with the numinous outside us. Thus it was natural to ascribe the divine attribute of immortality to it.

Plato too teaches (in addition to the two earthly forms of immortality through children and through eternal fame) an immortality only of the soul. When Plato later, from *The Statesman* on, expanded his psychology, he ran into the following difficulty: now he distinguishes between parts of the soul, and among them he distinguishes a genuinely evil part — whereas in the *Phaedo* evil stemmed solely from the body. Now if the soul as a whole is to become immortal, it follows that the bad part of the soul, though totally unworthy, will also become immortal with it. Yet the soul ought to become immortal only in divinely pure and good form! Plato does recognize two levels of immortality: on the one hand, the soul as such is immortal; on the other, the true and highest immortality is a reward only for the good. The soul of whoever lived unvirtuously on earth will be reincarnated as punishment. His immortality consists only in being incessantly reborn (and, as among the Hindus, men can be reincarnated in the form of animals). True immortality in a bodiless postexistence beyond our world is attained only by the good. Although they suppressed the bad part of the soul, it is a constituent of their soul as of every soul and so it participates in immortality, and that is a contradiction which Plato struggled with but was unable to resolve.

Aristotle avoids this contradiction by according immortality only to the rational, that is, the good part of the soul, and consequently limiting immortality to the man who has a rational part. Scholastic philosophy followed him in this. If Plato regards only a part of man, the soul, as immortal, for Aristotle it is only a part of this part, though the one he considers highest, namely, reason. But again this results in an inconsistency. What it comes to is that life hereafter consists in pure rational activity; ultimately this would mean that we can carry on only pure mathematics. Similarly in Plato the activity of the soul, once freed from the body, is limited to the contemplation of the idea, though with emotional overtones. And that has even been adopted by Christianity: contemplation of the divine glory, the vision of God is, besides music, the only delight of the blessed in heaven. Islam, by contrast, pictures the joys of heaven much more sensuously. But philosophy thereby has so altered the belief in immortality that its original religious meaning has been completely distorted. It transforms the immortality of a living person into that of mere reason, the elevation of being is made into one of knowing the truth, life beyond becomes a philosophers' heaven. (Analogously, Fichte, who sees action as the highest thing, has action continue beyond the grave.)

Just as philosophy fills its idea of immortality with its own content, it does this also with the idea of God: God too "is doing geometry" or because only the highest object is worthy of him he is engaged in "knowledge of knowledge" (Aristotle). And this also involves a loss of the original religious meaning. The "living God" has become the watered-down "God of the philosophers" rejected by Pascal. Both the subjectively and the objectively numinous are dissolved under philosophy's grasp.

Christianity, Plato, and the Hindus, however, have one thing in common: they all hold existence beyond to be purer and more perfect than existence in this world. Man reaches the highest stage only beyond. Therefore already in this world the beyond becomes a goal worth striving for. Earthly existence does not contain its own meaning, but it is demoted into a brief time of preparation and probation, while the center of gravity of life lies in the other world. For the Orphic cult and the neo-Platonists, the soul does not first reach the other world only after death, but it originally comes from there. It has only fallen into earthly matter or been cast down as a punishment and has been linked with matter contrary to its nature. All its desire therefore strives very intensely to free itself from this bondage and return to its true homeland, to reverse its emanation by a remanation. Earth is only its temporary place of exile.

These are unfavorable preconditions for an anthropology. Man here represents not an ultimate, not a final value, but to a certain extent only a caterpillar from which a lighter, winged creature is to wrench loose. His deepest hope aims for precisely the transformation of his humanity, and a form of transhuman existence. Anthropology applies to only a phase, not even the most reputable, of a more comprehensive fate of the soul. It is not independent but forms only a subsidiary discipline of soteriology (the study of redemption).

Homer, in contrast, found all glory and beauty in this life, compared with which life in Hades is limited to a pitiful shadow existence. Without power and reason, the souls to whom Odysseus goes down (*Odyssey* XI) lead a pitiful existence. Only the blood of a slaughtered animal gives them back the power of speech. And Achilles, the proudest of the heroes of Troy, admits, "I would rather be a poor wage earner on earth than king of the dead." By reducing the existence of the dead to a shadowy state, Homer not only lifts life into the light by contrast, but he also relieves the living of fear of revenants, a fear which cast its spell over all of early mankind. The custom of erecting a gravestone, for example, was originally intended, among other things, to prevent the dead from climbing out of the grave.

While Homer merely devalues life after death, the Old Testament goes a step farther and eliminates it completely. As the Old Testament in its rationality rejects the polytheistic myths of the gods, it does the same with the mythology of a transcendental dwelling and forms of existence of the soul (while Christianity, on the other hand, is more open to both forms of myth). This is all the more astonishing because the Jews lived for centuries in Egypt, where the cult of the dead was predominant. Only later, especially through the Cabala, with its Gnostic influences, do ideas of a life hereafter penetrate into Judaism, but never did they attain the position they have in Christianity or Islam.

But the Old Testament does not say that there is no eternal life. It simply does not speak of it. In modern times, however, the reemerging faith in this world has frequently stood in expressed opposition to faith in the beyond. The highest part of reality resides not in the eternal but in the glory of the transitory. Earthly goals, for instance, the perfection of one's own personality or of the social structure, are man's true goals. Life is not merely a preparation for another world, but it has an immanent value (*Sinn*) and ought to be formed with as much dignity, beauty, and richness as possible according to purely earthly standards. According to Marx, our earthly life is so desolate only because, in the hope that a better life awaited us beyond, we have neglected the possible improvement of earthly institutions. (Marx bases himself on Feuerbach's impious and crude characterization of religion as a "life insurance agency.") "I exhort you, my brothers, remain faithful to the earth and do not believe those who speak to you of supra-terrestrial hopes," so Nietzsche has Zarathustra (Prologue 3) proclaim his faith in this world. But the greatest documents of such a faith are the verses which Goethe (despite his statements to the contrary after Wieland's death) has the aged Faust speak:

> I know the earthly sphere sufficiently,
> We are barred from any view into beyond.
> Fool whoever blinkingly peers toward it,

Clouds thicken over the likes of him!
Let him stand firm and look here around himself!
This world is not mute to whoever is capable,
What need has he to roam eternity!
What he knows can be comprehended.
Let him behave thus all the days of his life:
When spirits spook about, let him firmly go his way.

Part 3

MAN AS A RATIONAL BEING
(Rational Anthropology)

CHAPTER 6

The Glorification of Reason

The Greeks as Discoverers
of Autonomous Reason

In the Bible, God forbade man to eat of the tree of knowledge under pain of sin. What God has earlier revealed and still proclaims by the mouth of his prophet stands higher than what we can learn by ourselves. And Christianity holds all our knowledge to be merely vain and fragmentary. "We now know darkly as in a mirror." Man's true virtues lie in religious feelings, in faith, hope, and charity.

With the classical Greeks we enter another world. They understand man, not by starting with God, but by starting with himself and his own intellectual gifts. For them he is the being that has reason. Thus the Anacreontic poems say: "Nature gave the ox horns, the horse hooves, the hare speed, but man thoughts." For Plato the power of logic is the highest part of man's soul, and the same is true for Aristotle and the Stoics.

Not accidentally the Greeks were the first to develop the theoretical aspect and to seek knowledge for its own sake. Solon, and Herodotus who says it of him, traveled foreign countries only "for the sake of knowledge." The considerable stock of knowledge of the Oriental peoples on whom the Greeks were directly dependent stood in the service of practical purposes (e.g., astronomy stood in the service of navigation, the calendar, and the art of prophecy). Only the Greeks, who consequently far excelled their predecessors, sought truth as an autonomous value not dependent on reflected light from any other. Therefore only they cultivated philosophy and science as autonomous cultural areas and produced the humane figures of the thinker and the scholar.

Like theoretical knowledge, practical knowledge also became an independent field among the Greeks. The ethics of the Bible is God-oriented; man ought to follow the moral commandments because they are ordained by God. Everywhere men guide their behavior by traditions inherited from ancient times and reverently preserved and taken for granted, for no one asks whether they can be justified by reason. The Greeks first established rational ethics: once man acquires such confidence in his own reason, he dares to disobey divine or traditional regulations and instead follow what his own inner voice dictates. Systems of philosophical ethics vary in content but all are based on one common principle: that man always ought to and should do the good which stands the test of his reason. (Actually he is always, and more than he knows, led by traditions; very often reason merely confirms the content of traditional good, so that behavior remains externally the same as before, but is elevated to a higher stage of legitimacy.)

Only the man who lives by his reason is a truly individual man. To obey one's reason means merely to obey oneself, to receive one's directives not from general traditions and rules but from one's own soul. Rational ethics is autonomous ethics, and even the unhindered development of theoretical reason presupposes an autonomous individual no longer bound by tradition. After complex civilization had brought about a certain independence of the individual which made Greek faith in reason possible, this faith in turn led to a still greater independence.

As newly discovered reason conflicts with tradition on the outside, it also has opposition within man himself, namely the other powers of the soul, the drives and passions (Max Weber distinguishes between three main motives of action: traditional, rational, and emotional). In Plato, reason, as the highest power in us, is supposed to rule over the desires. In the Stoics, reason is supposed, if possible, to completely suppress the emotions: motionless quiet of spirit (*ataraxia*) is their ideal. Indeed, Aristotle justifies tragedy because it effects a "cleansing of the passions." Kant still stands in the same line of tradition: for him ethical behavior is reduced to maintaining the supremacy of rational duty over sensuous inclination. As opposed to this, ethics since the Storm and Stress movement knows that the nonrational layers of the soul also have a necessary life function to fulfill. They cannot be completely suppressed, and even their suppression beyond what is absolutely necessary impoverishes life.

For the Stoics, reason—which stands for the total inner value of the person—gives not only autonomy but also autarky; that is, reason makes us independent not only of the emotions but also of the external demands of property and fate. "The wise man is sufficient unto himself." Even when he no longer possesses anything material, he may remain indifferent, for he still has what is more than material: himself and his virtue, which nobody can take away from him. *Si fructus illabatur orbis inpavidum ferient ruinae!* ("Though the world should collapse, the ruins would slay an undaunted man.") Herewith a previously unknown stage of interiorization is reached, and even Christianity therefore was later unable to absorb Stoicism. Life is not a matter of "earthly trifles" but of one's own soul and its purification.

Stoicism overextends and discredits its own principle when it not only teaches us to value interior rather than external things but also declares externals worthless and indifferent. Not everything nonspiritual is trivial. Not only do high secular values of culture exist—for are the Brandenburg Concertos a "trifle"?—but the soul itself can develop its full potential only by dealing with worldly things. Subjectivity and objec-

tivity, the internal and the external, cannot be separated. Only
by further education can my mind be refined; only by association with a friend do I blossom forth as a human being;
only by professional activity can I train and activate my
energies. If I am excluded from higher education, if I do not
meet my friend or he refuses me his friendship, if the pro-
fession for which I am talented is overfilled and offers me
no chance, then it helps little if I tell myself, like the Stoics,
that all this is only *Allotria* ("irrelevant trivia"), and the only
thing that counts is an upright character. When the externals
are missing, the interior lies fallow. This is indeed higher, but
it presupposes the externals as a foundation.

World Reason and Human Reason

According to an old Oriental concept, man contains on a
small scale everything that can be found in the cosmos. He
is himself a microcosmos.[1] Therefore the Oriental does not,
like the European, approach nature as a person different from
it. Unlike the European—who therefore historically pounced
on him like a beast of prey—the Oriental does not feel called
to dominate nature spiritually and technically (we discovered
the *motif* of domination already in Genesis). Thus all culture
ultimately depends on the concept of man. In Far Eastern
paintings man seems, to our admiration, to feel like a plant
growing in the landscape, like an integrating tone within the
great melody of the universe. And since he is only a part of
nature he can be understood by way of nature (later the
modern age reverses the microcosm idea so that nature—as
macranthropos—has to be understood by way of man. As-
syrian-Babylonian astrology was based on the idea that the
same event that takes place in the world of the stars must
also be repeated in the destinies of men. Even pre-Socratic
philosophy made general statements about being which
spanned nature and man in common (clearly the case, for

example, in Pythagoras); for the pre-Socratics, man did not constitute a special theme of philosophy.

That reason is the outstanding human characteristic does not necessarily imply that he has only reason or that reason gives him a special dignity that places him above everything else that exists. Though reason may place man above the animals, many hold that above man's reason there is a divine or world reason. For the Greeks, the world comprises an ordered "cosmos" governed by laws. This order, many assumed, can only have come about because a higher reason has ordered it planfully. This argument is still used in the physicotheological proof of the existence of God. According to Plato (and even Kepler!), the planets are creatures with souls, for otherwise how could they describe circles, that is, perform geometry, in their courses. That which is objectively in accord with reason seems to him necessarily to be subjectively rational. Following Heraclitus, the Stoics spoke of a world logos. As the Orphic mysteries depicted our soul as sunken from a higher kingdom of light, with which it had greater affinity than with the earthly, the Stoics regarded our human logos as a seed of the world logos. (Similarly Romanticism sees in every individual spirit the greater "spirit of the people" [Volksgeist].)

Thus man, even with his rational nature, could regard himself only as a "mirror of the cosmos." But the Greeks distribute the emphasis differently than the Orientals. Human reason is surpassed by a divine cosmic reason, but man's reason establishes his superiority compared with earthly things. As the only direct relative of the gods "not an offspring of earth, but of heaven" (Plato, Timaeus, 90a), man assumes a unique and incomparable rank among all other creatures. His relationship with the superior realm creates distance from the lower. As in Genesis he is singled out by his likeness to God, so for the Greeks he is singled out and elevated by his reason. This affinity made it possible for the Greek and the Biblical image of man to enter such a firm synthesis in Western tradition.

Scholasticism takes up the doctrine of man as a rational being as a preamble of faith.

If for Plato the thinking consciousness had been only the highest part of the soul, Descartes defines the complete soul as consisting only of consciousness. The soul, according to him, not only has consciousness, it is consciousness. He is thus the father of modern rationalism, just as Locke is father of the Enlightenment. Similarly Pascal states that man, though the universe may be crushing him, can point out to it something that he is which is greater than it: he is the weakest reed of nature, "but a thinking reed." Linnaeus too classifies man as the *animal rationale, homo sapiens*. "He distinguishes, chooses, judges" (Goethe). Exaggerated faith in reason did, in the Goethe period and in the nineteenth century, lead to a new anthropology which sees quite other faculties than reason as determinative in us. And yet rational anthropology still has not vanished completely. When man today is defined as "open to the world" in contrast with the animals, which are bound to their environment, rational anthropology is still alive in that thesis.

The combination of rational anthropology and a general metaphysics of reason also crops up in modern times. Reason prevails not only in the cosmos but also in world history, according to Hegel, who builds the traditional prophetic Christian philosophy of history into a metaphysics of reason. But whereas according to the Greeks a divine and perfect reason forms the cosmos, and whereas also in religion God already has his "plan of salvation" before history begins, German Idealism gives the idea a different turn. The world at first is based on a dull, unreflected reason without self-awareness. And the origination of nature as well as the process of history both serve merely for the self-development of the world reason and its gradual growth in self-awareness. The inorganic, the organic, and the cultural realm are merely stages through which reason, still lacking self-awareness, gradually progresses to greater consciousness and works its way toward the final goal of complete self-possession. Similarly in Plotinus (German Idealism is neo-Plotinism), the primeval oneness lacks self-knowledge: every knowledge presumes duality, an intelligent and an intelligible factor. Therefore the One splits and the entire ladder of hypostases comes into being by emanation (*proodos*) from it; but all stages are dominated by the desire to behold the One and return to it by contemplation.

Everything therefore contains reason, but only in a long climb does the still "dormant" reason—to use a word from Leibniz, who also belongs in this line of thinkers—intensify till it reaches ultimate brightness. Here German Idealism too, though differently than the Greeks, finds a way to accord a special place to human reason despite the rationality of the universe. It is not merely a reflection of the divine; indeed, even the divine can find fulfillment only in it. In human, especially in philosophical reason, the world reason acquires self-awareness. Therefore man ought, even in an emphatically moral sense, to be self-aware. He is the point in the universe where the secret primeval intention of the world process is being accomplished. As in the Bible, the last member of creation is its crown; indeed, creation was designed from the start for this late crown. The same finality of nature toward man is represented today in the much-read Teilhard de Chardin, for whom, however, man is only a transition toward the "noosphere" that is ultimately to be reached.

Reason-Nature Dualism

By virtue of his rational nature man ought to occupy the highest rank on earth. But not everything in man is reason. Spirit contrasts with body, thought with drive and emotion. Thus rational anthropology involves an anthropological dualism. As, according to Plato, there is a break (*tmēma*, "cut") between idea and reality, and as, according to religion, there is a break between God and the world, so a similar crack runs through man—or rather, the very same crack runs through man, since the soul is the part of us related with the idea and with God. The extrahuman *chōrismos* ("separation") is repeated within man. Man is a thoroughly earthly being, but by his reason he juts up into the upper realm. Dual in nature he participates in both realms and is exposed to the tension between them.

In Old Chinese writings man was considered a link between the heavenly Yang and the earthly Ying. Also in the Bible— which does not, however, deduce dualism from this—man is composed of kneaded earth and the divine breath (*ruach*). According to an Orphic myth, man originated from the ashes of the earthborn Titans, who had been struck by lightning, but who had first eaten Zagreus the son of Zeus and thereby acquired divine powers. The body-soul dualism developed by the Orphics still dominates almost all tradition since then, through Plato, who restricted soul to the part called spirit. Compared with Christianity it often seems as though the Greeks still lived from an unsplit harmony. Yet they were the ones who radicalized the split. Fostered by their philosophical and the Christian (and Gnostic) tradition, Descartes makes the two substances *cogitatio* and *extensio* so heterogeneous that they cannot even affect each other. Still they dwell in man near and beside each other. We are "citizens of two worlds" (Schiller); "drive" and "spirit" are joined in us (Scheler).

This leads to the conviction that dualism is only something temporary and that we will one day be redeemed from our suffering from it. Just as for Plato only the idea makes everything what it is, so basically reason makes us men, everything else remains "an earthly remnant to bear painfully." The spiritual became entangled in changeable matter against its nature. But it wants to, and will, free itself again from this entanglement. Our "dual nature" is a fall from our eternal essence, is already in this life something to be surmounted by battle against the earthly, and will be completely surmounted in death.

Man therefore seeks to delimit himself from the world around him, which he feels does not belong to him. The spirit is "like a stranger in visible nature" (Aristotle, *De anima* I. 4). Although proudly aware that he is destined by the spirit to be ruler of the earth, man feels uneasy, feels himself to be only a guest on earth because of the spirit. He has no permanent place here below and strives only "to escape from here to there as quickly as possible" (Plato).

We will see later that in the Goethe period and at present the theories of the two worlds have generally been overcome metaphysically and anthropologically. One does not escape dualism by emphatically taking one side and denouncing the other, but only by understanding the spiritual and physical in man from a deeper unity.

CHAPTER 7

The Dethronement of Reason

The Revaluation of Nonrational Cognitive and Psychological Powers

Sometimes reason is only another word for our faculty of knowledge in general; sometimes it is given the more restricted meaning of thought alone. The animal too has perceptive knowledge; in fact, some animals have sharper senses than we. But only man, as it is said, can achieve the highest form of knowledge, thought. Already Parmenides confronted perception as the organ that is not merely subordinate but illusory, with thought as the metaphysical organ. And Plato added to this a specification that survived to the threshold of the present time: unlike perception, which remains limited to the individual and the concrete, thought is conceptual knowledge, knowledge of the universal. Nominalism still taught this, though incidentally it refused to go along with the Platonic metaphysical treatment of the universal. Man is the rational being; that means here more precisely: only man thinks universal concepts. Descartes and Leibniz went even farther: for them, thinking is not only the highest but the only form of knowledge, indeed of any spiritual life at all. Therefore Descartes calls the soul *cogitatio*. Everything nonrational in it is only "confused thinking." Animals, since they cannot think, have no souls and are mere automatons.

Locke's empiricism opposed this type of rationalism: all our thinking begins with perception. Therefore animals too have knowledge and soul (the first animal psychology stemmed from the Lockean school); this does not, however, either for Locke or for Hobbes (*The Leviathan* 17), eliminate the chasm between animal and man (whereas later, e.g., for Schopenhauer, this chasm is narrowed by the fact that man is no longer seen primarily as cognitive but as emotional). In a direct reversal of Descartes, Locke even derives the concepts only from omissions of perception. But the genetic thesis does not imply a revaluation of the two. For empiricism too, conceptual thought remains the goal of all knowledge.

This changes only with Vico, with Baumgarten, Hamann, Herder, and the Romantics. For them, sensual knowledge no longer serves only for the preparation of the conceptual but is equal in rank—in fact, superior to it. For Feuerbach, the senses correspond to the previously despised third estate; as the latter attained equal rights in the French Revolution, now the senses are doing so. Since earlier "sensuality" was classified as a whole and since it was only a subordinate, preparatory stage, no closer distinctions within it were made. Herder was the first to investigate the specific accomplishments of the particular sensory organs. He is thus a precursor of modern esthesiology, such as that of Plessner and Katz. (Of course, Diderot and Lessing preceded him, the latter, in his *Laokoon*, tracing back the differing laws of literature and the fine arts to the fact that literature was meant for the ear, art for the eye.)

The upgraded valuation of our subjective sensuality is, however, only the result of a changed conception of the world of sensory objects. The Platonic-Aristotelian dualism, which has survived as a categorical framework well into modern times, distinguished between matter and idea or form. As deeply as matter stood below idea and form, perception also stood below thought. So it still was for Kant. But the pantheism that began in the Renaissance and made a renewed breakthrough in the Goethe period had opposed this dualism with a monistic belief. Everything real as such contains God and has a meaning. The meaningful aspects do not lie in a separate sphere of their own, but are immanent in reality itself. Thus reality rises in rank. And with it perception also rises. Perception, in grasping the real, no longer grasps merely amorphous raw matter but the divinity that resides within it. It is perception that grasps meaning. Indeed it stands even higher than thinking: for the meaning that is woven with reality into symbols is infinitely richer and deeper than the matter-free isolated abstractions that thought attains. The Goethe period therefore places aesthetic (no longer the thinker but the poet is the true man) as well as historical perception above nonsensory modes of knowledge such as philosophy and science, which had formerly held the field. That the Goethe period produces a golden age of literature and an awakened and broadened sense of history are two related facts based on the same ideological foundation. The poet, who moves in the sphere of individual things, and the historian, who does not seek to construct rationally the essence, e.g., of the state, but buries himself in the phenomenon of actual states—these two, who exhaust the living fullness of the concrete, are superior even as knowers to the mere representatives of reason. Their views open up mysteries that the pitiful, merely thinking reason will never be able to teach.

But not only perception is played off against rational thought. What was called thought in the eighteenth century was no longer the emotionally colored Platonic contemplation of ideas to which a realm of essences organized by form was revealed, nor Spinozan intuition in which knowledge of the world and of God coincide, but analytic, measuring, calculating thought and understanding that dissolves the world into a mechanical contraption made of quantitative particles and thus makes it technically masterable. The correlative of this type of thinking is only a "nature without God, without magic, without mystery" (Schiller). To this the answer of the Goethe period was: the world is not so poor and desolate, not "so gray, chimeric, deathly"—Goethe used these words of Holbach's *Système de la nature*. But in order to plumb its true hidden depth, one must not approach it only by thought or only by perception; to plumb it effectively man as a whole must step into action, including action with the deepest energies of his spirit, with his feelings. The profundity of nature responds only to the profundity within us. It is not so much thought as experienced. The feelings, recently discovered by Rousseau for the educated and by Tetens also for philosophical psychology, are not merely pale conditions of the subject but they have a world-discovering ("intentional," as Franz Brentano and Scheler expressed it) power. Early mankind, i.e., the primitive peoples, and the men of the Middle Ages, with their universally pervasive faith, who still breathed within full reality more than we rational men who have been made shallow by the Enlightenment, were therefore not merely underdeveloped and retarded, as was previously superciliously believed. On the contrary, we must admire and envy them: with their emotionality, with their intuition (a favorite word of the Romantics), with their visionary dream, they stood closer to the essence of things, the divine foundation of the world, than we do. But we too ought to strive, as far as it is still possible today, not only to train our understanding but to reactivate those more elemental strata of the soul (the "instincts," Nietzsche will say later) and so, as it were, to become once again "the first men." Reason is not the divine part in us! *Homo sapiens* is replaced by *homo divinans* (intuitive man). And the evaluation of human objectivations shifts accordingly. We have already seen that the Goethe period attributed a higher content of wisdom to art than to philosophy and science. It does this not only for the sake of sensuality but also for art's greater depth of feeling. For the same reason, religion assumes a place next to art.

The Goethe period sees not only feeling but also the subconscious as wiser than reason. This is a step farther away from rational anthropology. Along with perception and feeling, powers of awareness are also mobilized against the power of thought. Now, however, the consciousness as a whole is debased. Though man alone has consciousness, it is not to his credit. The best in man is not that he has consciousness, which separates him from other beings, but that he too is moved by the universal, unconscious wisdom of nature. "Man cannot long persevere in a conscious state; he must cast himself again into the subconscious: for there his root is alive" (Goethe).

The concept of the subconscious originated with Leibniz. But for Leibniz the subconscious was only a negative stage of awareness and not something positive. Every subconscious element struggles for awareness as its goal. Schelling and Hegel—as we have already heard—consider nature and history not the work of a consciously planning God, but of an unconsciously self-manifesting world spirit. However, the goal that the world spirit follows in this is self-awareness, and it attains this goal in and through man, who thus is distinguished by his mental brilliance, completely in the style of classical tradition.

The Storm and Stress movement and Romanticism, on the other hand, celebrated the subconscious as the more primary, the higher and more genuine element in man. The subconscious is at work on the outside, and also within man; indeed, the more it works in man, the more substantial he is. Awareness and reason are our misfortune; they choke out the natural subarticulate element in us and block us off from our deepest streams of energy. They lead us irremediably astray, never penetrate beyond the surface, and whatever they produce is always artificial. Only the subconscious creates intrinsically necessary works which mirror creation perfectly because they themselves are a genuine part of creation. Therefore according to Herder the greatest works of literature are folk literature, because the people still tend to create in the twilight of the subconscious. The individual, at least in late times, always stands in danger of writing only from the thin surface of the understanding. What he contrives remains stilted and shallow, without more serious truth content. Only if he is a genius can he still draw on subconscious sources, and, as it was formulated at that time, he will not only copy nature (*natura naturata*) but also imitate nature (*natura naturans*), for nature lives in him, and his production is therefore permeated with its wisdom.

These convictions were swept away in the nineteenth century by a new wave of rationalism and remained alive for only a few men—Carus, for instance. But in depth psychology they came forward mightily again. Freud, whose concept of the subconscious goes back to Leibniz (via Herbart), in seeking to purify the subconscious and bring it to light, discovers the peculiar, archaic-imaged "logic of the subconscious." For C. G. Jung, who has roots in Romanticism, the myths of the early peoples and the dream vision, both of which stem from the (collective) subconscious, represent the highest revelation even for modern man.

For the Goethe period the subconscious is highest not only because of its achievement of knowledge. It is highest also because, compared with sterile reflective thought, it constitutes the creative factor in us. Thereby a fundamentally different anthropology appears than the one we have been treating up to this point: man is called upon not so much for knowledge as for creative productivity.

Man is furthermore called to life in the full sense of the word. The subconscious is only a deeper layer within the psyche; but here a step is taken below the psyche as a whole down to the next lower level of life. Man's mission does not at all consist in gaining insights, whether merely rational or more essential. The Goethe period first placed life above spirit: "*Primum vivere!*" ("First live!"). In a manner almost anticipating vitalism, it sees life as the more elemental factor, whose rights must therefore be recognized. "The very best requires from us not headaches but heartbeats" (Hamann). In his sea-going diary Herder bemoans his youth wasted in scholarly writing: Schiller likewise mocks the "ink-spattering century," and Faust, who has assimilated all sciences, gives up the world of books in disappointment, casts himself into the whirlpool of events, and strides through all the heights and depths of feeling—"Feeling is everything!"—to experience what life is. Nietzsche continued these tendencies more radically. "Man means thinker: there's madness in it!" Man is not merely a "cold demon of knowledge," but, laughing and dancing, we ought to sweep away all spider webs of reason; the teleology of life lies only in ceaseless intensification of its own beauty and power. "The intoxication of thought yields to the thrill of life" (Gundolf). According to Nietzsche, not only does knowledge not intensify life but every excess of knowledge even lames and weakens life. We ought to be deeply glad of our ignorance, for "to err is to live." We should not pile up boundless and unselective knowledge, through which we remain interiorly barbarians, but only such as serves the development of life. The spirit ought not to grow wild, but ought to serve as a functional organ of the greater whole of life.

Basing himself on religious anthropology, finally, Kierkegaard contrasts speculation with existence. A truth remains indifferent if we are not serious about it, making it our own and choosing it. This too has flowed into the present.

The Dependence of Reason on More Elemental Strata of Being

To this point we have heard opinions to the effect that forces other than reason are more capable of knowledge and ought generally to be estimated more highly. But perhaps reason itself is not something autonomous but only a special manifestation of layers of reality that are prior to it and stronger, or at least it gets its direction and meaning from them. These strata could be sought within or outside awareness, in matter or in life, in the social, cultural, or traditional: reason always is determined by something alien to it. This common thesis was promulgated with varying instrumentation in the nineteenth century.

Materialism

Physical and mechanistic materialism seeks to explain not only the area of nonliving matter from which it is derived, but everything, by quantitative mechanical principles. Descartes had come so close to this theory, which stems from the Renaissance (and the classical atomism of Democritus and Epicurus), that he agreed with them on the area of living things. According to Descartes, insofar as we are members of the spatial world, with our corporeal nature, we are subject, as is spatial reality in general, to mechanical laws. Animals, whose existence is limited to space, are completely so. Borelli then sought to develop this more precisely: our body is a system of pumps and levers. But for Descartes, man consists of cogitation in addition to extension, and his awareness is governed by completely different laws of its own. Descartes is thus a mechanist of the living organism, not of the spirit; from one point of view a renewer of philosophy, he proves to be an advocate of tradition: he saves the immortal soul from the grasp of mechanics. His philosophy could become official because it opened the way to the introduction of mechanism in a manner that could not endanger dogma.

Thoroughgoing mechanism cannot accept this dualism. It seeks to be a metaphysics and must include the spirit too in its spatial and material total interpretation of the world. Man himself must be understood monistically; the emergence of the spirit is not something in principle new or beyond nature; it too is "only nature," only "refined nature."

This tendency was most crudely formulated in a book by the French physician La Mettrie, *L'homme machine*. He was persecuted for it in France, but no less a person than Frederick the Great called him to his academy and on his death held a funeral oration for him. Even what we call soul is for La Mettrie only thinking and feeling matter. Even the so-called spirit is only a certain kind of motion of a certain kind of matter. "Matter has something lowly about it only for coarse eyes which fail to see it in its most glorious works." Thus philosophy would have to be transformed into physics and the only scientist who deserves gratitude from his country is the medical doctor. There is no difference between man and animal; nature made them both of the same dough and only the yeast is different. That man has language does not constitute a fundamental difference; the animals could learn to speak, but they simply don't want to; like men, they also have ethics and social life.

Sharing La Mettrie's views are Baron Holbach, Mandeville in England, and in Germany later Moleschott and Ludwig Büchner (a brother of the author Georg Büchner): "The brain exudes thoughts as the kidneys exude urine."

It is not as matter, but by analogy with matter, that spirit and soul are understood by mechanistic psychology, which stands at a higher level and goes back to Locke, finding its foremost representatives in Hume and Mill, and is brought toward its perfection by Herbart and Fechner, from whom the experimental psychology of Wundt and G. E. Müller then finds its point of departure. As the outside world is conceived by mechanism as a space filled with bodies (in the seventeenth century one was still said to explain something "geometrically" rather than "mechanically"), so the soul is understood by these psychologists as an inner space filled with perceptions. Therefore certain expressions that go back to Herbart and were transmitted to Freud by his students use the spatial images of "threshold" and "narrowness" of the awareness, because of which some percepts are "repressed" into the "subconscious." As bodies in space attract and repel one another, so ideas are associated according to certain rules of association which correspond to the natural laws, in fact are themselves natural laws. Herbart's students boasted that he had achieved more than Newton with his mechanics of the sky, since the soul was much higher and more complex than the physical world. In the manner of the Goethe period our century again knows that the soul is not constructed on the pattern of the physical world, and therefore the psychology of association has been replaced by a "psychology of understanding."

Religious anthropology interprets man supernaturally from above: from his God-given eternal soul. Here, however, a naturalistic anthropology meets us from below: neither man nor spirit represents anything fundamentally different and new compared with nature; the same laws prevail in both. These theories of the type "x is nothing but y" are, however, as phenomenology taught, fundamentally false, because they overlook the individual content of the phenomena. They reduce it explicatively to something else instead of recognizing its specificity. They commit the error of "lacking stratification," to use a term from Nicolai Hartmann. One cannot understand lower strata with the categories of a higher one, as Plotinus seeks to understand everything by the spirit or Bergson everything from life. Nor can one understand the higher categories by those of a lower stratum; one does not catch sight of the "categorical newness" at each level. The mechanistic theory of mind commits the error of lack of stratification.

Biologism

The mechanistic despiritualization of man is matched by the biological. While materialism today meets with rejection, biologism still holds numerous strong bastions. We can distinguish between two forms of biologism. One is the exact counterpart of mechanism. As mechanism says spirit is only a form of matter, this form of biologism says: spirit is only a form of life. So Comte wanted to dissolve psychology into biology. According to Haeckel, man is only the highest development of organic protein.

Pragmatism. The other, more cautious form of biologism concedes that spirit is something different from life. But it is only a subsidiary organ of life. It does not contain its purpose intrinsically; its task is not, as the Greeks claimed, to discover truth as rich and deep as possible for its own sake. It is intended merely to provide life with sufficient orientation for it to move about purposefully and safely in the world with its help. All its truth is therefore designed from the start to meet the needs of life, in fact the criterion of truth is its "service to life." "We think in the categories of our actions."

For Plato the spirit comes from a higher world and has only temporarily incorporated itself into life. It has brought from that higher world the law that dwells in it: to strive for the truth. The mind considers it only a bother that it does not glide freely in eternal circles but is woven into the fabric of life; this lames and dulls its power and knowledge. Nonetheless even while imprisoned in life it knows many things correctly, including both matters irrelevant to life and the kind of truths by whose standard it seeks to govern life. Anglo-Saxon pragmatism (James, F. C. Schiller, Dewey) is the exact reverse of this view. For pragmatism, the spirit is completely an outgrowth of life and receives its directives from life. Even its most specific task, that of knowing, is performed only on assignment by life. This is far from limiting the mind in its activity; the mind strives for truth only because truth is vitally important, and therefore it also seeks only those truths which are vitally important. And whether these are truth in the strict sense does not concern the mind: it is enough if practice is satisfied by it (therefore "pragmatism"). The older, classical sense of truth as a faithful rendering of the object is illusory. With the classical faith in truth the classical faith in man also falls. *Homo sapiens* becomes *homo faber* (man the maker), who uses his intelligence only to test things for their useful characteristics, and to produce useful things himself.

Schopenhauer and Marx. Pragmatism can look back to an illustrious series of ancestors. Schopenhauer had contested energetically the idea that the world and man are, in their deepest basis, mind. In their deepest basis both are will (cf., however, before this the doctrines of Augustine, ibn-Gabirol, Duns Scotus, and Maine de Biran's *"Volo ergo sum"*—"I will, therefore I am"). It is the will that produces intellect as its servant, so that it may light the way for him who, though stronger, is blind from birth. Schopenhauer thus understands the intellect from its practical functions; it is only the "medium of the motives." Indeed Schopenhauer does not even genuinely orient it toward truth. The will needs illusions for its own intensification. Therefore the intellect dangles before it imaginary goals which, metaphysically seen, do not exist. The original purpose of the intellect is not at all knowledge, but deception. Schopenhauer thus knew and opposed Hegel's metaphysics of the spirit and the spirit humbug of the Hegelians, and he wrote angrily: "Spirit? Who's the fellow and from where do you know him?"

Schopenhauer's style has a strong time-conditioned similarity with that of Marx. Marx too turns against Hegel on this point: whereas according to Hegel awareness determines being, in truth being determines awareness. This corresponds entirely to Schopenhauer's conviction. Schopenhauer, however, is thinking in terms of individual psychology; for him the determining being is the will of each individual; that which is determined is his intellect. Marx, on the other hand, has the whole nation or culture in mind; the determining reality resides in the "material conditions of production," and their product consists of the spiritual, objectified constructions. But beyond this divergence further common factors also emerge. As the intellect, according to Schopenhauer, produces illusions in the service of the will, so for Marx all prior art, religions, and philosophy are ideologies that have no truth content but the sole purpose of sanctioning the economic and sociopolitical hegemony of the respective ruling class. According to both Schopenhauer and Marx therefore an unreal superstructure is erected over every real substructure. The supposed structures of knowledge actually grasp nothing real but are only schemes that originate from the needs of the supporting class and are meant to serve their interests. Marx coined the term "ideological superstructure" for this. All creations of culture are only the expression of socioeconomic facts and intentions. They are subject to what has been called "ideological suspicion." Subjectively philosophers may be honest and seek the truth in good faith, but without their knowing or wishing it, the class instinct will speak out of them; the concepts will take such shape in them and so depict things as the class interests demand. And the same is true of art and religion. Thus the church justifies capitalism, for as long as the lower classes still hope for a better life beyond, they will more likely accept their oppressed and scanty lot and not think of revolutionizing the distribution of property and power in this earthly realm.

Though Schopenhauer and Marx are precursors of pragmatism insofar as they underscore the partial nature of spirit within life as a whole, they cling to the classical concept of truth: the mind directed by the will and the class present not merely an orientation in the service of life, which limits the content of truth by the type of questions asked, but—since according to the classical theory of truth the influence of life only disturbs knowledge—"illusions" and "ideologies." Besides the mind that is imprisoned in life and deceptive, both thinkers recognize a mind that is freed from life and capable of truth. Thus despite their new insights tradition continues in them in a peculiar mixture. They reconcile in themselves two interpretations of the mind, by accepting two types of mind. One could therefore call them—and similarly Bergson and Scheler later—semipragmatists.

One may recall Aristotle who taught that originally, as long as man still had to fight hard with nature, because the most elementary cultural institutions such as agriculture, house construction, etc., still had not been invented, the mind had stood completely at the service of practical matters. Only when life became easier as a result of those inventions and men found leisure could the mind turn also to unnecessary occupations such as philosophy and science. Thus Aristotle already distinguishes practical (and indeed really practical and not only— as the Stoics and later Kant used the word to mean—"ethical") and theoretical reason. And though according to Aristotle the practical reason does not really deceive us, as in Schopenhauer and Marx, still it is inferior to the theoretical: only theoretical knowledge penetrates to the metaphysical essence of things and to knowledge of causes.

As for Aristotle, so also for Marx, the mind runs through two stages of development. According to Aristotle, to be sure, the second stage has already begun: men first had practical, then later theoretical knowledge. But then practical knowledge still retains its justification: both forms exist beside each other. According to Marx, however, the second phase lies in the future. Until today there always existed a ruling class and every mental production was therefore an ideological superstructure. But soon a classless society will arise and therewith a "leap into freedom" will result in the mind too. Once the mind has no socioeconomic positions of hegemony to defend, it will be concerned only with pure truth. The ideologies, however, will by then have run their course (just as for Marx's contemporary, Comte, the religious and metaphysical age will end once the positive age has begun). The start of the age of truth is for Marx not only a by-product of the all-important social reform, but both goals have the same dignity. Therefore in all socialism down to our day—more than in Fascism—there is a spark of reverence for the mind.

Marx builds the doctrine of the two forms of mind into a philosophy of history and a prophecy: one form of mind will replace the other in the course of history. Not so in Schopenhauer, who is alien to all historical thinking: the higher form of mind can make a breakthrough at any time in history. But while for Marx it is imparted upon all men, for Schopenhauer only a few succeed at it. Only in the genius and the ascetic saint does intellect escape from the rule of the will, cease dangling merely illusory goals before it, and become a disinterested "pure world eye" that penetrates through "the veil of Maya" to the metaphysical. But all great art which unveils and depicts the eternal structures of the world is the expression of an emancipated intellect not directed by the will.

Despite a certain parallelism in the line of reasoning of the two philosophers, Schopenhauer's thinking is more biologistic than is that of Marx, who remains more traditional. For Marx it is not in the nature of our spirit to produce ideologies. Our spirit does this only because and as long as a false social order forces it to. By nature it is oriented toward truth, just as in the classical view. And therefore as soon as the right social order has been established, this, its nature, which had only been suppressed and deflected, will emerge by itself. For Schopenhauer, however, the human intellect is not originally directed to truth. The will in fact produced it precisely as an organ of illusion. The intellect did not, as it were, come under the rule of the will, which imposes illusions upon it only by an external misfortune; rather, the intellect itself by nature seeks illusion. If it does nonetheless soar to intuition of essence, this occurs not merely as a revolt of the slave against the will but even as a revolution against its own nature, which is structured quite differently. Though for Schopenhauer knowledge of truth becomes the goal and the distinguishing mark of man (whom he once even calls *animal metaphysicum*), that is so only because of a revolution against man's own original purpose. Essentially man is no longer "born to see, destined to behold"; essentially he is a vital being.

Nietzsche. Schopenhauer has already proclaimed that the dominant force in us is not intellect but will. But Schopenhauer seems not yet to have had the courage of his own conviction. He decides to let us be not only capable of but even called to knowledge; indeed, supported by knowledge, we ought to kill the will. He already has a new anthropology but not yet the ethic that goes with it. This new ethic is first held by his more consistent disciple, Nietzsche. We cannot by any legitimate title oppose what constitutes our deepest nature; in fact, we must affirm it. If we are will, then we must also want will—or, as he says, life. Life, as we said above, has for Nietzsche no task beyond itself, but in itself: it ought to rise to ever higher power and beauty. Knowledge is neither its mission nor its talent. All products of the mind are only "symptoms" of the life that expresses itself in them. Even the supposed theoreticians stand "fatalistically under the spell of their instincts" and falsify out of the world-as-such the picture that they subjectively need. However, for Nietzsche as for Schopenhauer, truth is accessible to us. But Nietzsche's stance toward it is ambiguous. Sometimes he condemns it because it makes life sick, for life can prosper only in a foggy atmosphere of illusory concepts. Sometimes he demands it and reproaches all previous philosophers with lack of truth.

Like Kierkegaard before him, Nietzsche makes the discovery that involvement in life need not at all disturb knowledge, as Plato believed: vital interests can also stimulate knowledge, bring some things to its notice and pose problems for it. Scheler, above all, took this up and carried it farther. Even for the purpose of knowing we ought not to renounce life but ought rather to commit ourselves to its greatest depths.

How much our convictions come from life and are subject to its demands, Nietzsche showed especially for our moral convictions. In his *Genealogy of Morals* he distinguishes between strong and weak, ascendant and descendant life. From a sociological perspective this coincides with the distinction between rulers and servants. Even Nietzsche's biologism is—though not so exclusively as Marx's—a social biologism. Already the French socialists had (as had antiquity) seen that every society breaks down into two societies, and that in it an upper and a lower class stand opposed. Whereas, however, the socialists believe that this primal fact ought precisely to be overcome, in Nietzsche's eyes it has already been overcome excessively and ought on the contrary to be reestablished. Each of

the two strata now develops, according to Nietzsche, a morality that reflects its respective social position. The morality of
the rulers is a symptom of their will to power; the values of
nobility and prestige are dominant in it. In the morality of
"those who got the short end," however, moderation, gentle-
ness, pity are dominant: such virtues are meant to make the
lot of the suppressed to some degree bearable. But that can
succeed only if the suppressors too accept these virtues for
themselves. And that has happened: in Platonic-Christian morality "slave morality" has gained general acceptance so that it
seems today as if it were the only possible morality. While for
Marx the ideological superstructure always stems from the interests of the ruling class, for Nietzsche morality comes precisely from the serving class. Under their influence the rulers
have given up the "lordly morality," which would actually be
suitable for them. But now that they have realized how they
have let themselves be outwitted, they ought, according to Nietzsche, to return to it.

Freud. Marx traces mind back to the desire for possession;
Nietzsche, to the drive for power or, respectively, to the drive
of the powerless; Sigmund Freud, to a third great vital drive,
sexuality. His point of departure is Schopenhauer, whose will
already has traits of sexual desire. For Freud, libido is man's
prime mover. Even the "drive" for knowledge as it had already
been called earlier, though not with a naturalistic intention, is
only a side branch of the all-pervasive sexual drive. It stems
from the child's libidinous curiosity and longing for enlightenment about the facts of sexuality.

But not all our libido is conscious. To a great extent it functions only out of the subconscious. Our culture compels us to
deny our drives. The drives which we are not permitted to live
out in reality and often do not dare admit even to ourselves
are not therefore extinguished; repressed into the subconscious, they continue to exist. "Traumas" of the soul, too, sink
into subconscious "complexes." Our much-praised consciousness now is based completely on the more fundamental

subconscious and is directed by it as the stronger force. Generally, it is true, we do not know this and live subjectively in the belief that we are acting from rational motives. In secret, however, it is subconscious mechanisms and strivings that dominate our actions. Consciousness is only a rationalization of them. The essential reality does not at all take place on the surface of consciousness, but in the subconscious depths, which therefore have to be elucidated by "depth psychology," alone capable of curing illnesses of the mind. Splitting man into a nongenuine foreground and a hidden genuineness, psychoanalysis has an external stylistic relationship with existentialism that reflects their contemporariness.

Schopenhauer and Nietzsche had already revealed the maskedness and deceptive concealment of our life. Our century then wanted to smash the facades of the nineteenth century and return to unconditional genuineness. After we have gotten to know genuineness, we again admire the wisdom of the facades.

From the insight of Herder and the Romantics we have already learned that our consciousness has its roots in the subconscious. But they held that not all men are ruled by the subconscious in the same way. The late-born individual can lose contact with it. Only the early age, only the people, only the genius lives fully in it. For Freud, however, dependence on the subconscious is a pervasive human trait. Herder and the Romantics furthermore consider dominance by the subconscious a positive factor. For them, the subconscious is not only stronger than the conscious but also wiser and more valuable. Only the subconscious makes us productive, while consciousness left to itself remains sterile. According to Freud, on the contrary, the subconscious is stronger, but the conscious is higher. As a doctor he recognized how frequently the influence of the subconscious poisons and lames us. Therefore he invented his methods to free men from its harmful influences. What the Goethe period bemoans—that we can release ourself from the tutelage of the subconscious—that is

just what Freud strives for. C. G. Jung also made the valuation of the Goethe period fruitful for psychoanalysis. But he
too knows of the parts of our being that are still unintegrated
into our personality and constantly accompany us as "shadow"
and "dark brother."

Freud makes consciousness not only dependent on the unknown drive stratum; he also has it originate from it. The
mental has its origin in a "sublimation" of the drives, a term
already used by Nietzsche. The energies directed by nature
to sexuality, to which the goal is only partially conceded by
culture, seek other goals and are converted into religious,
philosophical, and artistic energy. The mind is only a surface
phenomenon of the libido, which masks itself behind it; only
a genetic product in which that libido is distilled. As such it
is, however, bound by its own law. For Schopenhauer, the
will produces the intellect as something substantially heterogeneous, but as its servant; for Freud, the mind grows out of
the libido itself as a spiritualization of it, stands therefore
genetically closer but can then remove itself farther from it
in its direction and the choice of its contents. But as to how
the transformation of the libidinous energy into mental and
cultural energy is to take place, Freud, like all genetic theorists
who explain higher things from lower, does not provide an
answer.

But perhaps he means only to say that mind, which may
have originally been present as an aspect of libido or outside
it, is tremendously intensified or grows, so to speak, beyond
itself—because libido conveys on it all its natural power,
which had not originally been meant for it, and pushes it
from behind on its own course.

The mind is thus directed by life not only in content; it
does not merely originate from it but also obtains its own
power, intensity, and *élan* from it. The drives give up their
own goal, i.e., themselves, to support the mind in achieving
goals of its own. Others have asked how the mind can hold
its ground against the forces of the soul and the world. They

answer: not as mind, but only if naturally more momentous impulses join it. They need not give themselves up at all; on the contrary, it is all the better if their goal coincides with the mind's goal and they cooperate not only with their momentum but also with their own finality. Already Spinoza set up against the Socratic-Stoic ethic, which claimed that reason intrinsically represses the passions, the counterthesis based on psychological experience: reason succeeds at this only if it can mobilize another passion against them, and itself to some extent becomes impassioned. Similarly for Marx, world-historical ideas take effect only if real interests stand behind them; otherwise they "foul up." (Following him, Max Scheler spoke of the fundamental impotence of the mind, and Nicolai Hartmann set up the general law of the world that the higher factor is always the weaker.) Marx already bases his view on Hegel's doctrine of the "stratagem of reason," which, however, transfers the idea from anthropology to metaphysics.

For Hegel the fact that men act not so much from knowledge as from passion is precalculated by the "World Reason." Therefore it so arranges world history that the great individuals who decisively move the process of events come into situations in which by a preestablished harmony they do out of personal interests exactly what Providence has planned. A military leader performs his deeds from ambition; but these deeds still propel the events forward in the intended direction and signify a step in the mind's movement toward self-realization.

Reason as the Enemy of Life

In the antique as in the modern mind-life theories, the mind knows what is right for life. If one of the two factors is encroached upon by the other, it is the mind. This delineation underwent a reversal by Ludwig Klages (and Theodor Lessing). Klages' love also belongs to life—he calls it soul.

But whereas the thinkers dealt with above ascribe to life the power of making mind into a pliable instrument and therefore do not need to debase it, for Klages the two are "essentially opposite forces." The mind (formerly the divine spark in us!) is transformed from our title to glory to our ruin and the quintessence of the negative. As an uninvited and unassimilable stranger, indeed an encroaching enemy, the mind invades the regions of the soul which are both more valuable and more vulnerable: with its activity of will it scares them out of their plantlike, changeless, happy slumber, and weakens and destroys them. All glory falls to the soul as the motherly basis of life that gives birth and nourishes; Klages does not see the naturally wild and destructive sides of the soul. On the other hand, on the side of the mind he sees only the coldly analytic, not the creative, formative spirit.

As in Manichaean-Gnostic speculations, however, the spirit-soul antagonism is not a necessary primeval antagonism of world principles. For Klages, too, evil rebelled against goodness only subsequently. His anthropology also expands here into a philosophy of history. It does not belong to man's essence to be visited with the sickness of mind from the start. Originally man was intact like all other animals, and only later (historically not even very far back—only with the Greeks) did his decadence begin because of the parasitic mind.

And man did not even provoke this decadence himself by a "fall into sin." Klages expressly states that no intrinsic reason can be discovered either for the genesis of the mind as such or for the point in time when it took place. It fell upon mankind like a natural catastrophe. And all the intellectual accomplishments of which mankind has been proud, the change from the symbol to the concept, from magic to technology, from the chthonic matriarchal law and faith to the father principle, all these things were really stations on the path of decline.

Rousseau had already called progress regression. The Storm

and Stress movement and Nietzsche regarded the increasingly rational culture as an undermining of man's substance. But for all of them the catastrophe is not inevitable. As for the Manichaeans light wins over darkness in the end, so mankind can turn back its previous development and plunge back into the healing original floods of life. Klages, on the contrary, thinks apocalyptically. The pestilential bacillus of the mind will corrode deeper and deeper into man and will finally kill him. "The essence of the historical process of mankind is the victoriously progressing battle of the spirit against life with the logically predictable end of the destruction of life."

But as little as we can understand man as mind free of life, so little can we understand man as life free of mind. Life is never merely unconscious existence; in however dull a form, it always contains knowledge of itself and of the world. Even the pre-mind men, Klages' highly praised Pelasgians,[1] therefore also had knowledge, in fact since they were not yet alienated from the great powers of the cosmos by the mind, since they were still at unity with them, they even stood closer to them in knowledge. They had a natural primeval knowledge, even intensified in visionary ecstasy, of the living and moving flow of the world and existence such as the static mind, which tears apart every continuum (Palagyi had said this earlier), will never attain. Klages, by keeping the primeval Pelasgian men free of mind, does not mean to deny them all insight; on the contrary. But the organ of this insight is the soul instead of the mind. "Mind," in his language, means only abstraction and calculation; it is concerned—in Scheler's language—only with practical knowledge, not with the saving knowledge that Klages affirms. But just this is what Plato and Spinoza had in mind when they considered man to be distinguished by mind. Klages' attack on the anthropology of spirit, or mind, is thus not at all directed against their great tradition and real meaning. He is taking a stand against the later debasement of their theory.

CHAPTER 8

The Accomplishments of Reason

Contemplation of Essences
and Classification

Till the beginning of our century, rational theory was influenced by Plato and Aristotle, whose doctrine of being divides all things into an ideal and a material factor. The ideal is the essential one, which makes each thing what it is. Matter only fills the essence with reality. To know something therefore means: to know the idea in it. Perception too always operates with ideas. The highest form of knowledge, however, consists in mental "abstraction" from singular reality, "putting it in brackets"—as the later phenomenological technical terminology called it—rising to the idea itself in its immaterial purity, from actual existence (*Dass-sein*) to quiddity (*Sosein*). This valuation is still preserved even by those who no longer ascribe a higher mode of existence to the ideas as world essences, but regard them only as concepts of our thinking—be they innate (aprioristic nominalism: Descartes, Leibniz, Kant) or concepts derived from perceptions (sensualistic nominalism: Locke). Following Husserl, Scheler celebrated "contemplation of essences" and the "act of ideation": only man, by ascetically restraining his natural drives and impulses which storm at reality, or by setting a hiatus between drive and action, as a negator, can temporarily deactivate the immediate impression of the reality of things and so discover the eternal content and meaning.

The essence of a thing is generally common to many things, to all things of the same "species." It is thus a "universal essence." Still, it can be won not only synoptically, by comparing numerous similar things, but as the phenomenologists and Scheler have shown, even on the basis of one single instance. By the example of a piece of wax Descartes grasps intuitively what a physical body in general is. Buddha, who as a king's son was kept far from all negative impressions during his childhood, takes his first independent walk into the city and meets a poor man, a sick man, and a dead man carried on a bier: at a stroke the true fate of men and his own task of helping them are revealed to him.

Things can also coincide with the nonessential. By recognizing the analogies between them—Bain sought to define genius as an exceptional ability to do this—one gains further general concepts. Each thing falls not only under the class of things that share its essence but under countless classes, to which it belongs only through peripheral and temporary qualities. Only by subsumption of the individual as a specimen under a general grouping do articulation, lucidity, and manageability enter into the sensually perceived world. Primitives and children live more in individual, mutually incommensurable percepts than in comprehensively higher conceptualizations.

Further achievements of reason are: (1) The logical linking of several concepts (subsumption, definition, conclusion). (2) As we have known since the Goethe period, contrary to Platonism, even individual knowledge does not stand lower in rank than conceptual knowledge and must, like it, be sought and especially trained. (3) Since Democritus and more strongly since the modern era the task is assigned to reason to know the causes of things and the laws by which they move and develop. As does the knowledge of individuals in historical science, so the investigation of causes in natural science leads further than conceptual thinking. (4) The animal remains bound to the given firm "shapes"; man has the capacity of analysis and synthesis; he divides complexes into elements and puts them together again.

Creative Reason

Our knowledge (both of the individual and of mankind) does not always already have possession of its objects. The scope and depth of knowledge can grow. Indeed, the objects of reason are not, as it were, given to it from the outside so that it need only open its eyes to see everything before it. In many cases reason itself must first, through its own activity, bring the thing to be known into view. It needs the preparation and the method to penetrate deeper and deeper into it. Since science is no longer only the administrator of a firm stock of knowledge but seeks to be living research or bold exploration into yet unknown frontiers, our reason faces tasks which it must master; in fact, even the discovery of such tasks is one of the mind's tasks.

The higher research stands, the more consciously it is controlled, the less it stumbles upon its objects, the more it finds them by virtue of its own immanent logic. Already Kant saw that all science gets its direction from beaconlike "rational ideas." It stands, for example, under the idea of totality: it wants to know things completely and therefore it asks of everything it knows whether it may not perhaps be only a segment of a still greater whole which it does not yet know. It stands, moreover, under the law of asking about the ultimate foundations and constitutive elements. Thus it goes on every side beyond what is already given. It develops "anticipatory schemata" which then only have to be filled in. And although it does all that for knowledge, i.e., in order to determine what exists, its behavior is not purely receptive; rather, it develops its own exertion and spontaneity.

That is true also for the approaching and solving of problems. In order to overcome difficulties of knowing, the scientific mind devises hypotheses and checks them critically against the facts until one of the hypotheses is confirmed by the facts. Thus, for example, Kepler advanced astronomy decisively with his hypothesis that the planets describe ellipses rather than circles. But although science needs the hypothesis for its progress, it cannot produce it only by a systematic methodology. The hypothesis that results in a solution always stems rather from an inexplicable "scientific instinct" or "scientific imagination."

Knowledge seeks to apprehend the factual; imagination rises above the factual and explores the nonfactual. But precisely for that reason it develops a fertility for knowledge too, for it leads toward new facts! That man is the creature most capable of knowledge is based not only on his much-praised ability for abstraction and his logic but just as much on the fact that he is the most imaginative creature. "For God linked it with us alone with a heavenly bond" and "Only he finds content who has something to add to it" (Goethe).

Receptivity also gains from that quality which is seen today as the primary human quality: creativity. Our reasoning power not only knows; it is also formative and inventive. We are unique not only because we have a comprehensive and objective picture of the world. We can construct a world ourselves and produce religion, law, art, in short the entire cultural sphere. *Homo sapiens* is just as much *homo inveniens* (man the inventor). And as knowledge, on the one hand, is the foundation of all cultural inventions, so vice versa the inventive mind is the basis for progress in knowledge.

The picture of man as a theoretician comes to us from the Greeks. Platonism sees behind everything in the world the archetypes and models that remain forever. All things are only earthly copies of eternal, normative ideas; all temporal process merely repeats the timeless essence. Therefore man's primary postulate is to absorb these ideas by contemplation. His action

is only their realization. ("Virtue is knowledge.") In late
medieval nominalism the ideas are cast aside. Thus the time
factor gains a completely new significance. Time does not
merely repeat temporal models, but it contains a productive
element. The process of evolution incessantly produces radically new things. This is true already within nature, which
always brings forth new forms and manifestations of life, but
it is even more true of man. Therefore he no longer sets
knowledge as his main objective, for he cannot discover patterns for his life anywhere, but can only produce them himself by his actions (already for Duns Scotus God had been
primarily a *willing* God). But by creating the general patterns
of culture, he decides at every point of history about the pattern of his own existence. Each individual too must on a
lesser scale again and again, and not only in the narrow ethical sense, decide originally about himself (this is a nominalistic
facet of existentialism).

Here the rough lines are given for an anthropology of a
totally different kind from that of classical antiquity. No
longer devotion to the object, but the spontaneity of the subject, equipped, as it were, with creative power and transformed from a microcosmos to a microtheos (small-scale god),
is primary; man is no longer characterized by participation
in the eternal and universal, but by variability and temporal
individuation. It is incorrect to contrast the modern philosophy
of knowledge stemming from the subject with antiquity's philosophy of existence. This is only half the picture. Knowledge
still belongs together with being as referring to it. The real
subject of the modern age is not the knower but the creator
(see Part 5).

Such drastic differences do not stem from the mental efforts
of the philosophers. To expect this of philosophy would be to
overestimate its capacity. It is the completely opposite basic
attitudes toward life of antiquity and of the modern age that
crystallize into these two opposite pictures of man. The pic-

tures are different because the great cultures that create them and find expression in them are different. Philosophy can only give logical clarification of the images of man that are presented to it by the great cultures, but then it does exert a retroactive influence upon the cultures.

Part 4

MAN AND ANIMAL
(Biological Anthropology)

CHAPTER 9

Man's Place in
the Animal Kingdom

Transition and Preview

Rational anthropology is dualistic. For though man has reason, he is not identifiable exclusively with it. A divided being, he consists of reason and the somatic physiology on which reason depends. Therefore two different groups of sciences are necessary to study him. This consequence, unsatisfactory as it may be, is inescapable. His rational side is investigated by philosophy, psychology, and the liberal arts (*Geisteswissenschaften*), his vital side by biology and medicine. Only when one, as it were, adds together the two groups of sciences does one have the whole man. However, the two halves are generally not considered to be of equal value. According to rational anthropology, it is reason alone that makes us men. Though the human body too is specifically human, still the real, specific property of man is supposed to be his reason. Human biology can now either submit to this valuation, or it can do what the nineteenth century did—claim that its half is of higher value and declare man primarily an animal. Reason too depends genetically or functionally on the vital side. Thus human biology tends to surmount anthropological dualism, though only on a naturalistic basis. Only the most modern human biology and psychosomatic medicine has succeeded, on the pattern of the Goethe period, in being monistic but not therefore naturalistic; it has achieved this by having man's physical and psychological faculties be geared to one another from the start, without giving primacy to either.

Therefore rational anthropology and biological anthropology also differ in respect to their determination of the relation between man and animal. Rational anthropology lets the same dividing line that cuts across man also pass between man and animal. As reason is the highest thing in man, it also distinguishes him from all other living things, whose intelligence cannot be compared with his.

Biological anthropology, however, has no reason to split the realm of the living and in principle contrast man with the animal kingdom, since man himself is not divided. Man is but one link in the continuous chain of organisms. Nor does his intelligence place him above the natural any more than, according to rational anthropology, the intelligence of animals places them higher than nature. Biological anthropology leads to the great counterattack against all dichotomies of both rational and religious anthropology, which are therefore classified together and historically were able to amalgamate easily because they both elevate man above nature by a trait belonging only to him.

The modern age (related in this with the Goethe period) has succeeded, after settling of the first excitement of the theory of evolution, in linking the two sides of man: for as it comprehends man himself in a nonnaturalistic manner as a unity, at the same time it places him within the unity of nature, without therefore surrendering his singularity or his special position. He still is contrasted with the animals (not only because of his reason, but as a whole), and this is so not by virtue of a higher consecration (i.e., because he protrudes into another realm, that of the supernatural), but by virtue of a structural plan of nature itself that is actualized only in him.

*The Bridging of the Contrast
Between Man and Animal
in Antiquity and in Modern Times*

Among primitive tribes, along with the higher ranking and deification of the animal we also find a feeling of superiority over it. Perhaps the taming of the domestic animal first made man aware of his lordship over nature and his fellowman and thus forms the basis of all higher technology and statehood. Psychologically the innate tendency of wanting to be superior, by which peoples also feel superior to other peoples, and individuals to their fellowmen, is the general pattern into which man's attitude toward the animal fits. What seems to be an insight is really the result of a predisposition.

On the other hand, the morphological relationship with the higher mammals and especially the apes has always impressed mankind. This was inevitable, especially when the explanation provided by the theory of evolution was still unknown. In early times therefore the question already came up about the criterion and distinguishing characteristics of man. These characteristics are called *anthrōpina*. Only man, it is said, for instance, walks upright, only he has hands (Diogenes of Apollonia, Anaxagoras). Or in view of external similarities with the animal the *anthrōpinon* is sought internally, for instance: only he knows good and evil and feels shame (the Bible), can laugh and cry (Plessner), can make a negative statement (Hans Kunz), preserves the past (Nietzsche), aims for the future (Buber), knows that he must die, is capable of suicide (Rosenzweig-Ehrenberg); or: only he can think, only he creates language, tools, and culture in general. We do not want to list pedantically the entire series. Most of the *anthrōpina* suffer from the defect that they or at least strong preliminary stages of them also can be found among some animals. Birds also walk upright on two legs; apes have hands

too and are curious (and perform practical jokes); bees—as
Karl von Frisch has proved—know language (e.g., communicate to each other, by dancing, the direction and distance of
a food source); both they and ants form a state (and Bergson
therefore compared them with man); many animals build
dwellings, etc. Taken as a whole, the distance is enormous;
but the individual theses on which it is built are generally too
particular and do not withstand the test of closer examination. Modern research has moved forward to the underlying
principles.

But the distance between man and animal is not uniform.
Not all animals are at the same distance from man. Some are
closer to him, some farther away. And perhaps the distance
between man and the animals closest to him is less than that
between these animals in turn and the ones farthest from him.
Let us juxtapose the infusorium as the lowest and most dis-
similar to man, the chimpanzee as the animal most similar to
man, and man himself: obviously in this series, the infusorium
and the chimpanzee do not contrast with man, but man and
chimpanzee are closer to one another compared with the
infusorium. The differences within the animal kingdom are
thus greater than the difference between the highest animals
and man—which does not exclude the possibility that this
difference too is a basic one.

At a very early date philosophy sought to lessen the emotionally drastic evaluative contrast between man and animal.
Plato in his *The Statesman* dealt ironically with the naïve
arrogance of contrasting the totality of other creatures with
ourselves under one concept "animal," when he said that this
is just as if one day the cranes got together and declared:
we are the cranes, the other living creatures, however, are
only animals (Gulliver has the same experience on the island
of horses). Thus Plato, like Aesop, has man see his own errors
in the mirror of the animal world. As in the *Theaetetus* he
unmasks the class mentality of the nobility as full of preju-

dices and vanity, so here he reveals hoministic arrogance. Of course Plato is thinking more logically than objectively. What does not apply to the crane might apply to man.

In his late period Plato is said to have once defined man as "a two-legged creature without feathers." (Frederick the Great appropriated this definition which seemed to confirm his misanthropy: he speaks of the two-legged unfeathered race.) In an anecdote, Plato's adversary Diogenes is said to have plucked a chicken and said: this is Plato's man. Therefore Plato added to his definition: "with flat nails."

Thus in Plato two different types of anthropology collide and are left standing, without interlinking or complementing each other: a zoological definition of man, which places him completely in the animal kingdom, and man's definition as a rational being, in which absolutely no mention is made of his animal side. This incoherent and unbalanced juxtaposition of two anthropologies is, however, a consequence of both a purely spiritualistic and a purely naturalistic conception, which mutually condition one another in their onesidedness. Therefore the juxtaposition has survived down to the threshold of our time.

Even as bearer of the mental equipment that contemplates ideas, man remains for Plato closely related with the animals: like the Hindus he allows for gradation from human to animal souls (and vice versa). Man is superior to the animals, as it were, only potentially: most men make but little use of their reason. As a penalty, after death they do not attain pure incorporeal immortality, but they must begin a new life. Yet the reincarnation of the soul in an animal destiny is no greater punishment than that in a human destiny, for according to The Statesman many souls voluntarily choose animal destinies.

Aristotle changes this: he no longer ascribes immortality to the entire soul, but only to its spiritual part and therefore to man alone. Only the spirit, which has entered nature from the outside ("through the door") as a heterogeneous higher principle and always remains a "stranger" in it, is divine and thus has a claim on immortality. Aristotle even associates the upright gait which he stresses, in his essay on the "Parts of the Animals," as a biological trait of man: man alone of all living beings walks upright, because his nature and his essence are divine (similarly Plato, *Timaeus* 90a). Even physically, man raises his head, in which the godlike reason dwells, upward in the direction where the gods live. Thus Aristotle, referring back to pre-Platonic thinkers, seeks to bring the animal and the spiritual in man into intrinsic interrelation.

Aristotle is the teacher of a unified world structure in which matter and idea are much less separate than in Plato. In his theory the realms of nature fit together, as later for Leibniz, like rising stairs, and the soul is even the entelechy of the body. Man is the pinnacle in the hierarchy of beings; that makes him tower above them but at the same time remain linked with them. Thus his decision remains in the balance. The ethically accentuated faith in the divine-spiritual special destiny of man, which has survived in Christianity, and the more metaphysical belief in the indivisible unity of the universe, which also includes man, both are retained.

Only in the eighteenth century, which in many ways undermined Christian dualism, could these initiatives of antiquity come to the fore again and develop anew also in anthropology. The most meaningful, effective, and epoch-making evidence of this is Linnaeus' zoological system, which first (though only in a later edition of the *Systema naturae* of 1766) assigned man a place among the categories of the animal kingdom and thus included him in it. Linnaeus placed man among the mammals as the first of the primates and called him—this famous designation goes back to him—*homo sapiens*. Thus even in biological anthropology the influence of the old rational anthropology continues. Here too man is characterized not by physical traits but by his reason and is thereby allotted a special position. He does belong to the animal kingdom—there is no separate human kingdom—but still he rises above animality by the fact that he is *sapiens* (intelligent). Therefore —and certainly also in reminiscence of the creation account that man was the last being created—man stands not at just any position in the animal kingdom, but at its summit.[1]

The Pantheistic Conception in the Goethe Period

For Linnaeus the doctrine that man and animal belong in the same classification is an immanent result of natural science. It presupposes the Enlightenment affirmation of this world, based on the spirit of the Renaissance, which resanctified nature and released man from exclusive orientation toward his otherworldly homeland. But only in the Goethe period did the teaching of Linnaeus (whom Goethe places alongside Shakespeare and Spinoza for his influence on him) become the expression of a new experience of the world and of man. Generally the Goethe period opposes the Christian God-world dualism with its own pantheistic monism. Therefore it also wants to overcome the man-nature dualism.

Thus Herder's *Ideen* ("Ideas for a Philosophy of the History of Humanity")—which despite this title is not only a philosophy of history but also an anthropology, except that Herder does put man essentially within the horizon of history—does not begin with its narrower theme, but with the cosmos, with the development of the earth and of life on it. Then man is placed within this comprehensive scenery; he is dependent on it not only externally, but the very laws of universal nature are repeated in him. Like the plant, he is subject to the influence of land and climate; with the animal he shares growth, procreation, and death. From the most varied aspects Herder tries to show how man grows from nature and how much he remains a growth of nature despite the incipient new element in him. "So little has nature created us as separate monoliths, as egoistic monads!" Man too is a rung in the ladder of life, and the traits of all other beings recur in him. Goethe tells that in the summer of 1830 he received a visitor with the words: "Now what do you think of this matter? Everything is in flames. It is no longer hidden behind closed doors. The volcano has erupted." The visitor of course thought that Goethe was referring to the July revolution that the whole world was talking about at that time. But Goethe denied this: "What do I care about that! I'm talking about the great dispute between Cuvier and Geoffroy."

Cuvier and Geoffroy were two French scholars of the time. Cuvier held the doctrine that the animal world is divided into four completely heterogeneous basic types, each of which goes back to a separate creative act of God. Thus for Cuvier even the animals are not firmly interrelated, how much less animal and man. Geoffroy St. Hilaire, on the other hand, held that the whole animal kingdom is an inseparable unity. This had always been Goethe's view. Geoffroy St. Hilaire himself had appealed to Goethe and Goethe defended him passionately in his quarrel with Cuvier. At that time Cuvier first won out. Darwin finally brought victory to the idea of unity in the special form of genetic unity.

Goethe, however, made a discovery as early as 1784 (without his knowledge a Frenchman had already preceded him in 1780): he discovered the *os intermaxillare* in man, which many called the Goethe-bone in his honor. And for him this discovery stands in the closest connection with his faith in the seamless unity of nature, from which man too cannot be left out. He made the discovery only because of this belief and at the same time he struck an argument out of the hands of his opponents.

The *os intermaxillare* consists of two small bones between the two halves of the upper jaw of mammals. The upper incisors are seated in these bones. For many higher apes and in man the seams between the intermaxillary bone and the upper jaws are often unrecognizable. Thus the intermaxillary bone does not appear to be a separate bone.

Now the anatomists at that time had exact knowledge of the thoroughgoing analogousness between the human and the animal body. But as heirs of religious and rational anthropology they shied away from an excessively close relationship of man and animal. Even the purely biological relationship, although the distance of mind and soul could remain unaffected, seemed uncanny to them. The apparent lack of the *os intermaxillare* in man seemed to serve their purpose. In all seriousness Camper still claimed that the essential difference between man and animal showed itself even osteologically by the fact that man had no *os intermaxillare*. What the connecting link between the true nature of man and this purely external little anomaly consisted of, one asks in vain.

Goethe found the supposedly missing bone. He compared numerous human and animal skulls and found that in skulls at the embryonal stage the boundary between the *os intermaxillare* and the jaws is still distinctly visible in man. The seam becomes obscured only after birth. In his treatise "Man like the Animals Has an *Os Intermaxillare*" he follows the intermaxillary bone in its changing forms through a series of mammals all the way to man.

But Goethe is far from desiring to lower man to an animal. He too believes in a special dignity of man. And in agreement with tradition he also sees this dignity in the intellectual and moral spheres. "Let man be noble, helpful and good! For that alone distinguishes him from all the beings that we know." Furthermore, Goethe himself had to assume that just as every phenomenon, in his view (after Leibniz), represents a "sensory-moral" unity, man too ought to represent one and thus express his intellectual difference physically also. But this difference cannot be limited to a single detail, a tiny anatomical difference. It would really be pitiful if only a small bone distinguished man from the animal. The independence of our nature must express itself in our entire appearance. "The harmony of the whole makes each creature what it is," writes Goethe to Knebel, "and man is man as much by the shape and nature of his upper jawbone as through the shape and nature of the last link of his little toe." The modern age has returned to this way of thinking.

But Goethe contests the absence of the *os intermaxillare* as a distinguishing *anthrōpinon* not only because it would be too slight a distinguishing trait but also because he could not believe in such a distinguishing characteristic. In his conviction nature constitutes a great unity which is everywhere the same though in various modifications. Therefore he does not merely describe the bone structure of the individual species of animals, but is from the start—like his French predecessor—a comparative osteologist (and in general a comparative morphologist). But it would contradict the unity of nature if the otherwise gapless analogy between the human and animal skeleton should suddenly fail at one point. If all animals have a special bone that holds the upper incisors, then man too must have it; they cannot grow on another bone just for him. His distinctive trait can, after all, not consist merely of a lack!

That would have seemed to Goethe like a debasement. The natural unity he believed in is a divine unity, its monism a pantheism. That man shares his natural accouterment with the animals had nothing repulsive or embarrassing about it for him; quite the contrary! Whereas earlier thinkers, for whom nature was a lower sphere compared with God, sought a trait that distances man from nature, Goethe in his reverence for nature was interested in finding precisely that nothing separates man from nature. Only as a link in the ring of nature does he share in its divinity.

Goethe's discovery has been cited correctly as an example of how empirical findings are made after ideological-intellectual anticipation. Goethe, as it were, saw the intermaxillary bone mentally before he saw it in reality. He found it because he was looking for it, and he sought it because this bone had to exist under the basic assumptions of Goethe's world view.

Therefore his extraordinary joy at the discovery. To his

friend of like convictions, Herder, who was at that time engaged in writing his *Ideen,* into which context Goethe therefore immediately fitted his discovery (though Herder did not accept it), he reports: "I have to inform you most quickly of some good fortune that has happened to me. I have found—neither gold nor silver, but something that gives me unspeakable joy—the *os intermaxillare* in man! See, there it is! You too should rejoice heartily at it, for it is the keystone to man, it is not missing, it is also there!" The discovery was for Goethe not just another contribution to man's bone anatomy, it confirmed anew and in contradiction to contemporary scholars his religiously toned conviction of the interrelationship of all living things. "And so again every creature is a tone, a nuance in a great harmony."

The specialists for a long time refused to accept Goethe's discovery, and Goethe was indignant about it. That he could not convince Camper, whose judgment he valued, drew from him the bitter retort: "A professional scholar doesn't surprise me when he denies his five senses." In the handbook of comparative anatomy by Blumenbach (1805) the human intermaxillary bone is still denied. Only in his old age did Goethe experience the acceptance of his discovery by science.

CHAPTER 10

The Theory of Evolution
and Its Opponents

Evolutionism and Naturalism

As closely as all organisms are, for Goethe, interrelated, and
as readily as man too fits into their series, Goethe did not
deduce from this that the various species of animals have
evolved from one another or that man came from the animal.
He conceived the relationship purely statically as a corre-
spondence of the visible and did not ask about its cause.
Or rather he saw it as stemming from the fact that nature is
everywhere subject to the same laws. He did let Thales—
not accidentally a pre-Socratic, for whom everything "came
to be" from something else—say in *Faust:* "You move by
eternal norms,/ Through thousands and thousands of forms,
and you have time until man." And yet this means only that
the forms arise in succession and not from one another. We
ought not to read later evolutionary ideas into these verses.
That man appears only after the animals was already known
in the myth of the six days of creation. And Buffon had already presented the modification that man was separated
from the animals not only by a single day but that life existed
for immeasurable ages without him having any part in it (and
even this seemed to many a degradation of human history and
culture). (By modern calculations man came into existence
only in the last two-thousandth part of total geological his-

tory.) But that man's kinship with the animals goes back to a common descent, that they develop one from the other and that finally man too developed from them as the last creature, this transition of thought from merely morphological similarity to genetic development, from the *post hoc* to the *propter hoc*, is an achievement only of the nineteenth century, of Lamarck and above all Darwin.

For Goethe the similarity of organisms goes back to their common mother, nature, which here still stands behind them like God in religion. Only immanent causal thinking has the organisms produce one another, i.e., derives the morphological context from the genetic. Such an interpretation was formerly militated against both by the Biblical dogma of creation, according to which God created all species of animals right at the beginning, and by the Platonic realism of universals, according to which likewise the species preexist unchangeably as eternal ideas, prior to all process. Only when, in the nineteenth century, faith in the Bible had declined and the nominalistic mode of thought had gained ascendancy could the idea that there is an "origin of species" (Darwin) make any headway. For the older style of thought an "origin of species" would have been the greatest paradox, for the species were defined as primary and eternal realities, as what "always remains the same" (Plato). Only radical nominalism made evolutionism possible, just as it had earlier made possible modern causalism, which no longer asks about the "essence" of things, about their eternal origin, but about the temporal, natural cause behind them. While Plato sought the truly permanent reality behind apparent change, the modern age seeks the real changes behind the apparently permanent phenomenon.

Only recently have scholars become accustomed to thinking in the enormous spans of time necessary for cosmological and biological transformation. Formerly the Biblical chronology, according to which the world was created only 6,000 years ago, was still believed. In so short a time, indeed, species of

animals cannot evolve one from another, any more than we
see them evolve before our eyes. Work with geological epochs,
with millennia (already Buffon) and finally with millions of
years began only gradually. This insight into the true depth
of time is the necessary correlative to the insight that the static
picture of the world, as our own narrowly confined experience shows it to us, in which everything remains the same,
is deceptive, and the insight that, seen as a whole, everything
is in constant movement and transformation.

Analogously, philology during the eighteenth century had
called attention to similarities between the Persian and the
European languages; but as children often do not know that
the similarity between relatives is based on descent, so
philology was satisfied with establishing the comparative similarities. Only in the nineteenth century did Bopp, reinforced
by Romanticism, which converted everything into history,
establish what amounted to a philological theory of evolution,
recognizing that the similarities between languages are family
resemblances caused by a living relationship and filiation.
Languages are not inherently and unchangeably static; they
develop and are derived one from another in the course of
long periods of time; especially the correspondences between
the Indian and the European languages suggest the assumption of a common original language. Thus in philology at the
same time as in geology, a short time before Darwin, the same
progress was being made. It is as if a new possibility of
thought had reached maturity and was now being adopted
by various sciences. Already in 1783 Lord Monboddo had
presented both the thesis that Greek and Sanskrit have a common origin and the thesis that man is an ape without a tail
and the ape a man without speech (which earned him the
ridicule of Dr. Johnson).

Compared with Plato and Aristotle, of course, even the
pre-Socratics were evolutionists. As cultural philosophers, they
were the first to believe in self-produced human progress; and
as natural philosophers, Xenophanes, e.g., knows that in many

places where land is, there must earlier have been sea, and vice versa. Biologically, Empedocles knows a successive zoogony. And Anaximander even knows an anthropogony: man must have come from another animal, for, if left to himself from the start, he—needing such long mothering— would never have survived. The theory of evolution, which aroused such a storm of outrage for churchly and dogmatic reasons in the highly enlightened nineteenth century, was thus already presented in the sixth century B.C. and not contested at that time. Through Epicureanism, which is based on Democritus and thus on the older natural philosophy, and especially through Lucretius' great didactic poem *De rerum natura*, knowledge of the evolutionary manner of thinking survived even in the Christian centuries.

But when the idea of evolution, which had been repressed by Platonism and the dogma of creation, was reawakened in the nineteenth century from a 2,000-year slumber, it was fused with modern mechanism. Therefore the turn that Darwin gave it represented something new. He was not, as has been falsely claimed, the founder of the theory of evolution, but he was the first to develop it mechanistically. Not the idea of descendance but that of selection is his achievement. For what sets evolution in progress? And why doesn't it always stop at the same level, but is an upward evolution producing ever higher and more differentiated species? Earlier times would have resorted to the efficacy of teleological forces which always strove toward an objective and had whatever was new already in mind as a goal from the start. Darwin, however, explained evolution causally and mechanically. It is not pulled from the front, but pushed from the back.

Already at the beginning of the century Malthus had taught that within mankind a "struggle for existence" prevails. For every "place under the sun"—to use a later expression—there are more and more aspirants waiting. Since the earth's population is steadily increasing, while on the other hand the living space on earth remains constant and can nourish only a limited number of people, the unequal struggle can only be ended through birth control (Malthusianism). Such a struggle for existence now also prevails according to Darwin in the animal kingdom. Each species of animal multiples more abundantly than the external living conditions (and its enemies) permit. Of a pair's progeny only a few survive.

Darwin combines this chain of thought with another. Each new generation is never an exact copy of the old, but small changes of organic form are always taking place. These do not follow a law or a plan, but happen purely accidentally, because nature can never repeat exactly the same thing. Darwin now connects this with the fact that only a few survive. Who survives is far from a matter of chance. Rather, those whose changes turn out to be useful to life survive. Those whose changes hamper life perish (a thought which Empedocles pronounced). And because the fittest survive and propagate and because successive small changes pointing in the same direction accumulate, there now develop, according to Darwin, not only better and better adapted animals, but gradually even higher and new species. If we regard the final outcome, then nature is to a great extent purposeful; therefore we are inclined to assume that a conscious intention is at work in or behind it. In reality, nature is purposeful without intention. The purposefulness arises through unconscious blind selection, and by natural selective breeding caused by the fact that of the variations that arise accidentally and without plan only the suitable ones survive.

Modern criticism of Darwin has recognized that the mere accumulation of accidental individual variations cannot suffice as an explanation of the origin of species. Obviously in the transition to a new species many coordinated variations that lead to the same goal take place at the same time. Modern biology therefore speaks of a "structural plan" of its own that each species has. Besides purely evolutive thinking a revolutive thinking has appeared, which posits creative new beginnings within the microevolution of the gradual transitions.

It is also highly questionable whether the higher species develops because it is better adapted, for first of all it would never, as Nietzsche already objected, develop from a merely passive tendency; secondly, precisely the higher being is the more endangered.

In the later nineteenth century it was usual to cite Goethe as a crown witness of Darwinism. Especially Haeckel regarded him as a precursor of his own monism. This much is right, that Goethe too believed in the unity and inner relationship of all living things. But the monism of Rousseau's and Goethe's time was pantheistic. It worshiped nature reverently and experienced it as spiritual and imbued with meaning. The Darwinian and especially the Haeckelian monism, however, was mechanistic. Nature in it was limited to matter. When therefore Goethe places man within the entirety of nature, he gives him part of its divinity. Goethe has absolutely no intention of combating the old faith in the divinity of man; but he extends this divinity to all of nature. When, however, Darwin and Haeckel put man in nature, man thereby becomes for them "only" nature.[1] Nietzsche spoke up against the careless paralleling of Darwin and Goethe:

> To set Darwin next to Goethe
> Is a breach of majesty,
> The majesty of genius!

Darwinism and Its Victorious Campaign

Already in *The Origin of Species* (1859) Darwin had left no doubt that the laws by which new species develop can also be applied to the origin of man. But as a pious Anglican he formulated, in all caution, only: "Light will be thrown on the origin of man and its history." That, as was later popularly said, man comes from the animal, specifically from the ape, first appears only in *The Descent of Man* (1871). In the '70s many others, such as Huxley, Vogt, and Haeckel, began to draw the consequences of the theory of evolution, also concerning man. "Anthropology is a part of zoology" (Haeckel). This, then, is the real "Darwinism."

Man too, it is now known, shares with all other animals the fact of originating from another species. The exciting similarity between man and, especially, the ape rests on blood relationship. "In tremendous distances which the mind can never fathom"—and it doesn't matter whether it was hundreds of thousands or millions of years—man must have originated from animal ancestors and prior forms. In view of this, however, the assumption (now disproved) seemed inevitable that the separation between man and animal had previously been exaggerated, that what they have in common far outweighed and that man basically was "only an animal."

This Darwinism concerning man had an unusually intoxicating effect in the last third of the nineteenth century.[2] It was no longer only a matter of scientific biologists, but wide circles both of the educated bourgeoisie and the proletariat (eager for a new world view) snatched it up and made it the core of a revolutionary movement. Books such as Haeckel's *The Natural History of Creation* and *The Riddle of the Universe*,[3] which today seem shallow, because in them the problem of man is narrowed down to only the question of his origin, went through incredibly high circulations. The entire mentality of the time seemed brilliantly corroborated by the theory of evolution and at the same time meaningfully symbolized and illustrated by it.

Nietzsche too, though he frequently spoke out against Darwinism, was inspired in part by it for his ethical concept of the superman, conceived in the 1880's.[4] His *Zarathustra* is to that extent colored by the time it was written in. He expressly says in it: "You have gone the way of the worm, and much in you is still worm. Once you were apes . . ." As man is a super-ape, so he in turn is "something that must be overcome" by the superman, who constitutes the extension of the road already covered into the future and to yet higher things. Man's species is not constant; he is "something fluid and malleable—one can make whatever one wants out of him." Just as every being till now brought forth a higher being, man should do the same. "Like an embryo of the man of the future," he is "not a goal, but only a way, an incident, a bridge, a great promise." However, what becomes of him is, in only his case, no longer a matter of nature: he must be his own breeder.

More conservative minds did not want to be robbed of their faith in man's spiritual nature. Especially the church had to oppose a doctrine that contested not only man's special position but also the creation of beings by God and instead had them originate through mechanical causality. But in their first horror the opponents found hardly any solid counter-arguments and went grumbling helplessly back to mere dogmas.

Darwinism was all the more successful because it fully accorded with the causal, genetic style of nineteenth-century science (while today, since phenomenology and *Gestalt* theory, a descriptive morphological, structure-revealing style, complementary to that of the nineteenth century, has again come to the fore). It was not only the natural sciences at that time which exaggerated the knowledge scope of the causal category ("to know is to know the causes"); even in the liberal arts the question of origin and influence was dominant. The concept of evolution seemed to be a magic word that caused all the closed doors to spring open. Specifically the higher was supposed always to develop from the lower, the differentiated from the simple, the spiritual from the natural. This is not a necessary part of the content of the idea of evolution: a thinker like Plotinus lets the lower come from the higher. The nineteenth century, on the contrary, put the idea of evolution at the service of naturalism: the idea of evolution presented a welcome opportunity for it to reduce everything to matter.

In this tumult of naturalistic inductive reasoning, the theory of evolution was seen as the cornerstone of the whole edifice. It allowed man, who had been standing by as an unaffected spectator of the general development, to become a part of it. He and his intellect no longer constitute an exception; he too is only the last product of the evolution of matter as its organization becomes ever more refined. *From the Speck of Fog to Man, From the Bacillus to the Ape-Man*: such book titles are typical of the times. They manifest joy that the world formula of evolution never fails, that the circle closes, that the lowest and the highest stem from a common—purely material—principle. As in other cases, such derivations of everything from one thing hardly ever fail to have a seductive effect on the understanding. Only by toilsome self-discipline can we educate ourselves to stand by the idea that the world is based on a multiplicity of principles.

If man had felt superior to all nature in religious and rational anthropology, now he is submerged almost indistinguishably in it. His mind too is only a refinement of matter. The pendulum swings from one extreme to the other, from arrogance to self-abasement. The peculiar thing is that men at that time did not regret the loss of this exceptional position —though it is not only a philosophical construction but also the expression of a natural tendency of feeling—but on the contrary they greeted it with joy. Their faith in the universal material unity of nature was so fascinating that they were even willing to accept their own dethronement, indeed they were proud of their humiliation. Haeckel expressly condemns the "anthropistic megalomania" that had prevailed till then. Man is only a "tiny grain of protoplasm within mortal organic nature." Theodor Fontane captured the mood in which the theory of evolution was propagated: "I was a witness of that affair with the apes, the theory that some orangutan or other was supposed to be our grandfather. You should have seen how glad they all were! When we still stemmed from God, there was nothing doing with us, but now that the theory of the apes became fashionable, they danced as before the ark of the covenant."

It must be admitted that the decades of Darwinism's propagation are the decades of the *Kulturkampf* (cultural struggle) and the "Away from God" movement. Not only was socialism —such as Marx's—antireligious (whereas today it has become indifferent to religion); the natural sciences too, as they gained strength, more and more dissolved the possibility of credulously accepting the myths of the Bible in good conscience. In this situation Darwinism seemed a welcome ally. It brought a positive element into the previously merely critical attitude toward religion: Darwinism itself was to become the new faith, destined to replace the faith in God. *Moses or Darwin* (Dodel-Port) was, despite its shabbiness, a much-read book at the turn of the century. This is a further reason why men were so easily ready to accept the removal of their privileged position by Darwinism. Opposition to the religious and humanistic world view that had become incredible included a reversal of the human self-estimation it contained. For satisfaction at disarming the enemy, people accepted the self-abasement that was entailed.

The deepest root for Darwinism's victorious acceptance, however, is psychological. Every culture makes demands on us. To be a man is never merely something that comes naturally. We must always overcome ourselves in order to maintain the standards set by culture; we must exert ourselves to satisfy our own expectations and those of others. As indispensable as culture is, still it does violence to us. This leads to what Freud has called the *"malaise* of culture." Deep in man's interior slumbers a grudge against cultural coercion that he would like to throw overboard like excess baggage, in order to plunge back into a more relaxed life. In vain! By the very fact of being men we are inevitably cultural beings. Hatred against culture is basically human self-hatred. To give up culture is to give up our own self. Nonetheless something

like a feeling of relief always goes through mankind when a
theory appears that promises to lighten the burden of being
a man. Hence the echo that Rousseau's call to "return to
nature" found in the eighteenth century; hence the success
that the totalitarian systems, which relieve man of his personal
decision and responsibility, have gained in our century; and
hence too the success of Darwinism. Finally man seemed to
be relieved of the pressure of *noblesse oblige*, finally he
seemed to be permitted to let himself fall off the steep summit to which he had elevated himself, for, thank God, we are
really only apes.

Two Types of Anti-Darwinism

Of the criticism leveled at Darwinism in this century, none
gained such a widespread temporary hold on the general cultural awareness as that of the imaginative, romanticizing natural philosopher, Edgar Dacqué, which could hardly be called
scientific. According to Dacqué, the theory of evolution is even
thoroughly right in mantaining that modern man comes from
another being. But this other being is not an animal. It is also
a man, but a man in another form. Man too has gone through
the whole series of phases of the animal kingdom; he too was
fish, amphibian, etc., but he was it from the start as the special being, man. Thus Dacqué succeeds in retaining the theory
of evolution, yet avoiding its consequences concerning man.
The animals did not merely develop and finally produce man;
rather, he himself originated together with them and existed
from the start as a primeval genus separate from them. But
this human genus too evolved, along with the animals, from
the lowest rungs of the organic up to the mammal. According
to Dacqué's most famous book, *Urwelt, Sage, und Menschheit*
("Primeval World, Legend, and Mankind"), a memory of
those early stages of our existence is even preserved in stories

of dragons and magic creatures. "What a spectacle! but alas, only a spectacle."

Klaatsch and Westenhöfer discovered another line of thinking for simultaneously accepting the theory of evolution and turning it into its opposite. Man comes from the animal only externally; seen more deeply however the animal comes from man. For Westenhöfer too there existed a *homo ante hominem* (man prior to man), but only virtually, as an idea. By the end of the age of amphibians the idea of man had appeared in the organic world—as in other times other ideas appeared. But this already circulating idea did not immediately find its adequate realization. For the longest time, the attempt to realize it in its purity failed again and again. And the result of this ever-repeated attempt is—the higher animals. The whole development is basically development toward the goal of man, by way of steps of failures till it was finally reached. Man did not therefore stem from the animals, but quite the opposite: the animals originated on the road leading to man. They originated by being left behind on this road, deviating from it and so falling back into the animal kingdom. Man, in the process of becoming, as it were, released the animals from himself. They are by-products of the anthropogenetic process. Although they precede man in fact, he precedes them as a possible goal.

Both theories do avoid the embarrassment of our animal evolution, but only at the price of a high degree of speculation. The scientifically productive advancement beyond Darwinism came from another direction. While giving full recognition to man's animal ancestry, which is no longer denied by anybody and no longer needs to be defended against any dogma, scientists began—in accord with the morphological propensity of our century—to pay sharper attention to the differences between man and animal. The findings were that the differences are so fundamental that in view of them man ought to console himself about the ancestral relationship. The whole dilemma—either man comes from the animals and therefore he is an animal himself, or he is from the first something different than the animals and has no connection with them—this whole dilemma is no longer a problem. It has been overcome by a third possibility.

All development has two sides: it lets the old continue to exist in the new and at the same time it transforms it into the new. The nineteenth century, which thought in terms of physics, here laid the stress on the preservation of the old: everything remains, only the form changes. The origin of a thing decides its nature. That man evolves from the animal therefore seemed to indicate that he himself was still an animal. By this one-sided understanding of the idea of evolution, the nineteenth century, which was always talking about that idea, cheated itself of its decisive dimension. Today the accent is placed on the productive aspect of evolution, on the new things it leads to. Its final result can contain what was not at all anticipated at its starting point. Therefore we need no longer deny the origin of the higher from the lower or even have the lower stem from the higher. What evolved from the low is not therefore simply a modified low thing, but can by virtue of genuine transformation constitute something incontrovertibly higher. Compared with the astonishing novelty that enters the world with man, that which man and animal have in common recedes to the background. What they have in common is not an animal nature but an organic nature that neutrally encompasses both man and animal, which each has developed in different directions.

Because we know a "creative evolution" (Bergson), we no longer are engrossed, as was the nineteenth century, with the idea of progress toward a goal viewed from which all less progressive stages are merely low and negative stages. Rather, it is a source of scientific pride in our century that we have learned to operate pluralistically in all fields with the category of equally valid types, none of which may be measured by the other. Though the "community" may have evolved into society (Tönnies), or the style of "drawing" into that of "painting" (Wölfflin), etc., this is not a progressive development. Whatever went before also has its own unique significance; and what came later does not merely perfect what was already contained in it, but it too strikes ahead in a completely new direction. The phenomena no longer can be classified in a line, but each one stands by itself. Therefore today research of the evolutionary, causal type has declined sharply.

This is true also of man's relationship to the animal. It does not merely represent progress. Both are completely heterogeneous types, perfect in themselves, objectively not reducible to one another. Therefore man is not bothered anymore by the fact that his genetic roots are in the animal kingdom. The question of descent is no longer for him "the question of all questions" (Haeckel). Much more important is for him the analysis of his own present nature as it has developed and is. For the same reason we also understand the animal today better than ever before for its own qualitative structure and laws, for we regard it not simply as a preliminary stage to man. But in the mirror of the animal we then understand man better too.

Modifications of the Theory of Evolution

A first significant observation is that the similarity between man and the ape is no longer as strongly pronounced with the adult ape as with the baby ape. Skull, hand, and foot are still manlike in the young animal; on the whole it has less hair and less pigment, and above all it is more intelligent—more curious, readier to experiment, more capable of learning than the old animal, which is much more firmly stuck in unalterable ruts of habit.

This already refutes classical Darwinism, or at least popular Darwinism, on a decisive point. The evolution that led

to man cannot at all have progressed by way of the finished
ape, for man holds firmly to a condition that represents only
a transition stage in the ape, beyond which the ape develops.
The consequence, at first surprising, is obvious: not man but
the ape is the one that evolved further.

It was always believed that man must have something that
the animal did not have. Our physical half, although specifically human, was seen simply as our animal half. What elevates us to men—that was only reason, which was added ex-
traneously to our animality. "Unhappy middle thing between
angel and beast!" (Haller.) This same way of thinking continued at first unnoticed in the theory of evolution. Obviously
the animal too has much that man is lacking. Man is not an
animal and then something else in addition, but the much
deeper difference is revealed by the fact that in other re-
spects he is less than animal. The evolution to man can therefore not consist merely in a further development of the animal; rather, it must subtract something from it.

In view of this new state of knowledge two possible ways
of thinking open up to the theory of evolution. Some assume
that already the generic idea of the Primates (the zoological
name for the whole family to which ape and man belong) has
more hominoid, i.e., manlike, than anthropoid, i.e., apelike,
traits. The ape branched off from this primeval form and
therefore embodies it only in youth, while man, although he
originated empirically later, still holds firmly to it. The organs
of the ape are much more one-sidedly specialized as if in a
dead-end street, while man displays a more primitive, archaic
form. Even so he had to pass from the animal-man stage in a
long process of hominization—from the "pre-hominines" via
the "eu-hominines" (Heberer)—until he reached his final development. And yet our origin from the animal kingdom thus
seems at least somewhat mitigated. ("Every age has the ape
it deserves!") Incidentally, contemporary ethnology is also
converging with physical anthropology toward the convic-

tion that mankind's beginnings are to be set not as deeply and coarsely as possible, but as high as possible.[5]

Under the leadership of the Dutch anatomist Bolk, others have held the descent of man from a "real" ape. In support they adduce the additional hypothesis of so-called retardation. From unknown reasons—perhaps because the climate became rougher or because of a failure of internal secretory glands—according to Bolk the normal development that leads, in the ape, from the immature structure to the mature structure, is retarded in man, i.e., slowed down or, rather, held back completely. He too grows and reaches adulthood, but structurally he preserves even as an adult the phase that is really supposed to be only a childhood phase. Before his development can progress according to its own innate law beyond this phase, he is already grown up. What is only a transition phase in the ape, thus becomes permanent in man. Man is, to put it bluntly, an infantile ape for which greater growth does not take place and which stays at the infantile or even embryonal stage. Such retention of immature traits (called neoteny) has also been observed in some other species of animals.

CHAPTER 11

The Human Structure

Unspecialization

Not only the ape but the animal in general is much more specialized in its general constitution than is man. The organs of the animal are adapted to the particular living conditions and necessities of each species as a key is adapted to a lock. The same is true of its sense organs. An effect and domain of this specialization is also the animal's instincts, which prescribe its behavior in every situation. Man's organs, however, are not oriented one-sidedly for certain actions, but are archaically unspecialized. (This is true also of man's nutrition; his teeth are neither those of a plant-eater nor those of a flesh-eater.) Therefore he is also poor in instincts: nature does not prescribe to him what he should do or not do.[1] Therefore also, for example, he has no special breeding season, but can love at any time of the year. Antiquity had observed this and looked upon it as a proof of divine favor.

This seems at first to be only a disadvantage for the progress of life. Such a creature will find it harder to maintain itself in the world than animals especially adapted to their environment. Hence the theory that man's development could have taken place only under "paradisiacal" environmental conditions. But, though unspecialization may have negative effects at the start, in the long run it means an invaluable advantage.

Lack of specialization turns out to be the negative correlative of a highly positive capacity. Because man's organs are not narrowly tailored to a few life functions, they are capable of multiple uses; because he is not controlled by instincts, he can himself reflect and invent. Therefore in exchange for the lack of one, he has the other. The specialization he lacks is more than compensated for by the fact that his multiple capacity and his own initiative enable him to adapt to changing external conditions and to make his existence easier through inventions and social institutions, so that he even far outpaces the animals though they seem to be better equipped for the struggle for existence.[2] In a novel manner, then, rational anthropology turns out to be right. "Reason" turns out to be the necessary correlative of unspecialization.

Protagoras, and later Herder, called attention to man's lack of specialization. The question however is how man's complementary positive abilities are connected with it. In our time Arnold Gehlen called man a "deprived being" because of his unspecialization. But one could just as correctly, balancing plus and minus point by point, also call the animals "deprived beings" because they do not have man's gifts. Therefore they were formerly understood, so to speak, as imperfect preliminary stages of man. Gehlen's concept merely reverses this line of thinking. As it was formerly believed that *the animal has no reason, and therefore he lacks something,* now it is said that *man has no specialization, and therefore he lacks something.* This whole method of understanding and evaluating one phenomenon by another has been overcome in principle in all fields by the modern typological mode of observation. Every phenomenon has its intrinsic meaning and can only be understood in and of itself. Man and animal seem to be "deprived beings" only as long as they are compared with and measured by one another. Then each one lacks what is admired in the other. But seen intrinsically, the supposed defects (Herder had already seen this) are not at all defects, but each lives through purely positive though opposite and incompatible capacities. That the capacities of one do not exist in the other is so far from being a defect that, on the contrary, for each to have the other's capacities would only interfere with the development of the respective species' own particular capacities.

When Gehlen further shows how man makes up for his physical deficiencies by the specifically human psychological abilities and how wonderfully the two intermesh, this is a naturalistic line of reasoning. He places deficiency at the start; man's intellect then develops as a compensation.[3] Man is not understood as an original totality from within, but his primarily negative natural foundation, precisely because of its negativeness, allows for the development of mind as a secondary trait. First nature endowed man scantily; compared with the animals he was a far less favored creature. But then man himself managed to make the best out of his scanty equipment, by letting his knowledge and inventiveness grow. The gap in his nature was precisely what became productive, releasing abilities that he would never have developed otherwise; for their place would already have been occupied by other abilities.

It is only a step from this to Theodor Lessing, for whom man is a defenseless weakling, disadvantaged by nature, an outsider and a dead-end street of life. The spirit and its accomplishments—tools, concepts, language, sociability—are always pitiful surrogates with which man compensates for his inherent weakness and manages to master life. And now he is even proud of all this—"the weakest creature is the proudest" (Montaigne)—though it only consists of artificial correctives, complicated detours, substitute routes that he must take because of his inadequacy for life. For Klages, whose ideas were similar to Lessing's in many things (because both drew on the same boyhood philosophy), man, inherently capable of health, was subsequently befallen by the sickness of intellect, but for Theodor Lessing man is essentially and incurably sick. Similarly Rousseau had called man "a depraved, corrupt ani-

mal" and Nietzsche "a sick animal." "The earth," it is said in
Zarathustra, "has a skin. And this skin has diseases. One of
these diseases, for example, is called man." The difference is
that, for Lessing, the intellect is the improvisation that keeps
him alive despite his disease. That man as a whole is not sick
but that, on the contrary, sickness makes him intellectually
sensitive and productive and that this dubious origin does not
at all militate against the intellect, is a frequent theory from
Lombroso to Alfred Adler, for whom intellect is overcom-
pensation for organic deficiencies, and Thomas Mann, for
whom disease is the yeast of culture (cf. Chesterton's criticism
of the concept of mental health). Ultimately the concept that
to be a man is to be sick goes back to Augustine.

Only man's lack of specialization is, according to this theory,
"nature." The powers that keep him alive are added to it
only as a compensation. But why should nature not have designed man as a whole? And why should nature not also have
planned those higher faculties of experience and creativity
from the start? He was not dealt with scantily, but completely
differently than the animal. His unspecialization need not be
the cause, it could just as well be only an effect: only because
he is designed on a completely different principle can, indeed
must, specialization be lacking in his case. It would be of no
use to him. It would only bother him. He is far from missing
it; it would even contradict his basic conception. Instead of
first being declared a deprived being, then having his deficiencies counterbalanced by advantages, he must be understood as a specific, self-contained type, in which everything
is simultaneously coordinated by structural laws.[4]

The contrasting of man and animal thus retains its justification despite the genetic relationship. Man and only man actually has a different structure than all the other animals, which,
compared with him, are all similar as specialized instinctive
creatures, whereas he lives from a new kind of aptitude.

By their specialized organs and instincts the animals are
restricted to very specific external conditions of life, within

which alone they can survive. Holistic ecological biology today
is giving special attention to these functional contexts. Each
species of animal has a specific living space (habitat); many
can live only deep in the sea, others only in underbrush, etc.
Within their own environment the animals move with complete security. As soon, however, as a change of conditions
occurs, a change of climate, exhaustion of a feed source, the
appearance of new enemies—as must happen over long periods
of time—the animals often cannot withstand the change—and
the higher they stand, the less capable of it they are. It is true
that animals too are capable, within a certain scope, of learning by experience and of adapting their way of life. Especially
under the influence of external change, which here turns out
to be a productive factor, new species are formed that are
adapted to the changed conditions. (Some thinkers admit of
only this adaptive creativity in the entire organic realm, while
others, e.g., Nietzsche and Bergson, also believe in a spontaneous creativity, a self-change without external necessity,
caused only by pressure of internal abundance.) Nonetheless,
regionally or planet-wide, entire species of animals became
extinct because they kept their stereotyped, unpurposeful
habits and could not abandon them even under new conditions. Their specialization, so much to their advantage under
normal conditions, then became a fatal liability. Perhaps this
—in addition to the exploitation of objective living conditions
—is one reason why nature produces so many different varieties with differing habits within each species: if one perishes,
the other has a chance of survival, and so the whole species
is saved from catastrophe. But man, because the unspecialized
is more adaptable and therefore has more chances for the
future, is more resistant to catastrophe than the higher animals.
This is because of a new method of meeting catastrophes. For
he is no longer subject to the tyranny of species-bound living
habits: he determines his habits himself. Things exist for him
not only under the perspective of their utility for purposes of
one single form of existence, but—much more many-sidedly

—so that under other forms of existence he can use them for other purposes. Within every culture man does tend to follow a uniform mode of life. But he is not restricted to any one of these modes of behavior. As he himself has designed them, he can also redesign them. Therefore he has no single environment, alone suitable for him. In every new environment he can develop behavior suitable to it and preserve himself in it. He feeds himself now by the hunt, now by fishing; he builds his huts now of wood, now of stone, now of snow. But this means further that changes in the outside world affect him far less than they do the other higher animals. To survive he need not change his whole biological nature, but he can merely change his external living style along with the external conditions. Therefore he is the only animal that was able to propagate over the entire globe, for wherever he goes, he adapts to the existing conditions. He is at home at the poles or at the equator, on water or on land, in the forest or on the plain, in the swamp or in the mountains.

Here we can refer to the basic categories of Arnold Toynbee's cultural philosophy (cf. also Winwood Reade). Again and again nature and history compel us to face "challenges." Nations and epochs differ only because some have become "fossilized" in their living habits and therefore incapable of mastering the challenges meaningfully. Only the "creative response" of others lifts culture out of the stagnant repetition of identical patterns to higher forms of behavior. When the formerly green area of the Sahara became arid, a part of the peoples who lived there wandered southward where external conditions similar to those they were accustomed to still prevailed and where they thus could continue living as before. Others remained there but changed their way of life so that now they could maintain themselves even under completely changed conditions in the desert. Thus they were more creative; but still they were merely adapting. A third group, on the other hand—the Egyptians—came upon the idea of using the water and mud of a river, the Nile, to make the land fertile themselves. That was more than a response to a challenge. The challenge became an incentive for a perfectly new idea that went far beyond mere reaction. However, excessively hard challenges, such as those of the Eskimos, can cripple the creative impulses from the start. It must still be added that man can, as it were, also challenge himself. Even without the pressure of an external challenge his overflowing creative ability can lead him to a change in his way of behavior.

If one wanted to become lost in speculations, one could venture the supposition that "nature's real intention" in producing man was precisely to create a being that can adapt to the most varied and unpredictable environmental conditions, or rather, since the purely passive "adaptation" of the nineteenth century is no longer sufficient, can control them, and therefore has much higher chances of survival compared with other beings. This would—on this purely speculative plane—also elucidate why man appears as the last and only being of this type on earth: after he is there and with him the survival of life seems assured, there is no need for further experiments with life. It would also explain why he is not divided into varieties: the ability to withstand catastrophes, which the animal species seek to achieve with the help of varieties, he achieves with the help of "creative response." What the animal achieves with the different varieties, man attains with his various cultures, which to a certain extent replace varieties. Nature's tendency to creative multiplicity and renewal, which in the animal manifested itself on the level of organic forms, continues, in man's cultures, on an intellectual level.

The Rhythm of Growth

Two conclusions can be drawn from the above remarks. First, even man's physiognomy is a specifically human physiognomy. This may seem evident to an objective mind. But rational anthropology and the older theory of evolution that

was dependent on it had a tendency to regard the vital sub-
stratum of man as practically that of an animal. The really
human side was believed to begin only with the intellectual
superstructure. Deepened insight, however, has now rediscovered that even the biological in us is totally human. Man
differs from the animal from the first by a comprehensive
structural principle that also includes his physical side and
expresses the human already in it. He is not divided into
human and nonhuman layers.

Secondly, the physical and mental qualities of man are not
unconnected with one another. They are not merely two
separate spheres or strata, one superposed upon the other.
Each is oriented to the other, and they condition each other
mutually. This particular physiognomy needs this particular
rationality as its complement, and vice versa.

It is therefore in principle inadmissible that, as we showed
in the introduction, two different sciences, one a natural science of anthropology and the other based on the liberal arts
(Geisteswissenschaften) should split man, as it were, into two
halves, parallel but unconnected. The science of man must
be a unity, as he himself is. Methodically and for the division
of labor it may be justified to some extent to go separate ways
as before. But human biology and the anthropology of the
mind (Geistesanthropologie) must, as parts of one science
of man, each include knowledge of the other as part of their
background. Only so will each understand its specialized field
in terms of the whole, and interrelate it with the whole, and
the artificial separation between life and spirit will be bridged
from both sides.

An outstanding representative of such a procedure from the
side of human biology is Adolf Portmann. Portmann not only
describes the inner coordination and interpenetration of the
somatic and the mental in man, but unlike Gehlen he is even
inclined to give the mental the primacy in this coordination.
"It is the mind that builds itself a body!" The mental is not
added to the somatic as a complement, however necessary and

suitable; the somatic is already determined by the primary
mental principle and can only be understood in terms of it.
Many physical aspects in man have to be arranged differently
than in the animals because they must coexist with a mental
reality.

As Portmann partly discovered and partly systematized, man
is distinguished from the other mammals not only visibly but
in a different rhythm of growth.

First man would have to spend a much longer time in the
womb by analogy with the other mammals relative to his size.
He comes to the world almost a year too early and so gains
an "extra-uterine year." Therefore the human offspring, as
Anaximander, Pliny, and Herder had previously observed, is
so helpless.

Next man requires a great deal more time until adulthood.
As he adds something to his childhood backward by being
born earlier, he also adds something to it by extending it
longer. He grows until after his twentieth year, that is, even
beyond the age of puberty (whereas a whale reaches its full
size of over sixty feet in two years).

Within this much longer growth span, man also follows
another rhythm than the animals. First he grows twice as
much in the first year as the nearest related apes; he practically catches up with the growth they have in the embryonal
period. Through this intensive growth of the first year the
brain—whose mass in man today is three times as great as
in the apes—can develop at an early age. Furthermore, in
mammals the strongest growth also lies at the beginning, in
the embryonal period and in childhood, and gradually de-
clines until adulthood. Man, however, does grow analogously more slowly at first, from the second to the ninth year:
in this entire period together he likewise grows only about
double as much as in the first year alone. But that is not a
gradual decrease until maturity as in the animal, but from
the tenth to the sixteenth year the growth curve suddenly
rises sharply again: in this period he grows twice as fast as

in a year of the preceding period. And only when this "puberty growth" is over does human growth steadily decline till it stops completely. Thus there are two high points, between which lies a long wavy valley. (Similarly psychoanalysis has discovered a sexuality of early childhood that likewise does not increase in a straight line until the full sexuality of the adult stage: in between lies the asexual, so-called latent period.)

This human childhood period, which is lengthened in both directions, stands in closest correlation with the special mode of man's total life guidance system, and is meaningfully oriented to it. The animal is guided in its behavior by natural instincts. Therefore it can spend a long time shut up in the womb, where the instinctual organization matures by a purely biological process. After birth it needs no long childhood; the instincts come out by themselves. "The order of their actions is woven into the whole species, but is not the property of a single individual of these animal creatures" (Buffon). Man, however, is guided by the mind. This is true both of the subjective mind of his own person and—at first in fact this is stronger—of the objective mind of the whole group in which he grows up, of the culture that varies from group to group and represents the solidified sedimentation of former subjective mind. Culture is man's "second nature." But each individual must first grow into this culture, must assimilate it by learning. Cultural customs, language, mores, technical skills, etc., are not preformed, innate capacities that merely have to develop like the instincts. Man has only one innate capacity: namely, to learn all this; only one instinct: that of imitation. In this regard he is more apelike than the ape. He must first, in his own process of assimilation, accept and practice the cultural traditional lore of his group.

Therefore the early birth of man: as soon as possible, while he is still as malleable as possible, he should already be in contact with his social companions, and the cultural norms which he must adopt should act upon him. Even something

as elementary as his upright stance and gait is not based only
on a hereditary, inborn disposition, but also on the influence
of the example of adults on the child, and is therefore not at
all present from the first (while young mammals manifest the
stance and walking position of their species from birth or
almost from birth). The first age of man is not a "chimpanzee
age"; he does not have first to overcome the ape in himself.
From the very first he grows, matures, and moves according
to his own laws (even the ratio of white and gray matter in
the brain is already different in the newborn infant than in
the animal).

Therefore also his long childhood: the appropriation of
culture is something so difficult that he must not only begin
early with it but continue with it for the extraordinarily long
time that is necessary. It is not enough to know the cultural
institutions and habits purely as such. One must as it were
become familiar not merely with the cultural vocabulary but
also with the cultural syntax. It takes a lot of effort to penetrate this complex apparatus and to use it meaningfully. One
cannot become acculturized as if by instinct and without a
contribution of one's own.

Even for the mastery of culture itself man must train his
subjective intellect. He must do so simply because again and
again he will face unforeseen situations for which there are no
adequate cultural norms of behavior and in which he therefore must independently modify the existing norms or invent
completely new ones by himself. And for this in turn he must
have an overall view of the things of the world; he must perceive them in a much more comprehensive sense than the
animal does. Man's understanding must do two things simultaneously: penetrate into culture and the world and at the
same time develop independence of thought. A man must have
brought all this to a certain perfection before he outgrows the
protection of his parents. And even in the adult stage he always needs a certain childlike gift of learning and self-perfection, which may therefore not blossom forth in him like a

quickly wilting flower but, because he must rely on himself for many years, must remain anchored in his life right to the end. Therefore a late maturity is not an accidental anomaly from which culture originated as it were out of a play instinct. On the contrary, it is dependent on man's destiny for culture. Both are harmoniously composed for one another. Biological and cultural-philosophical anthropology intermesh.

The length of the adult stage must stand in a corresponding ratio to the long childhood. As man is young for a long time, so he must have a long adulthood in order to bring up and instruct his own progeny. Therefore man becomes older than any of the animals related with him, for which, in accord with their earlier maturity, the opposite process of aging also begins much earlier. Smaller mammals live only for a few years, middle-sized ones twelve to fifteen years; and only a few animals get to be more than thirty years old; fifty-year-olds are exceptions. Even the anthropoid apes are old at twenty and begin to decline; only in a few cases do they outlive their thirtieth year. Man however can become seventy years old and even older without showing signs of senility. Folklore about man living longer than the animals crystallized into the legend that he originally was to become only thirty years old but that on his request God gave him further (more burdensome) years. The ratio of adulthood to youth in man still remains shifted comparatively in favor of youth. Youth occupies a relatively greater portion of the entire life of man as compared to the animal. By analogy with most mammals, man with a twenty-year youth would have to become over one hundred years old.

Furthermore, while for animals age means decline and decay, man's life still remains at a relatively high level and meaningful despite sinking vitality. When physical energies recede, the mental can remain intact; indeed, "the sight of our understanding becomes sharper when the sharpness of our eyes begins to decline" (Socrates, to Alcibiades). Even after he has reached adulthood, man does not merely preserve what he has acquired in youth, but he remains an "eternal youth" (this could in turn be associated with the "persistent childishness" and rejuvenation of the domestic animal) insofar as he can acquire new external and internal experiences in a much broader scope than the animal. "As I grow older, I am still learning much" (Solon). Man attains the wisdom and serenity of old age. Many artists even develop a productivity of their own in old age, and their creations then reveal a new "old-age style" that deviates from their previous manner and shows the world in a completely different way. This is now being made the subject of special study in the history of art and literature.

Openness to the World

The specialization of the animals also extends to their organs of knowledge. Their knowledge moves only within a narrowly delimited specific "environment" (Jakob von Uexküll). Their subjective specialization thus, as it were, meets an objective specialization of the world, and both specializations intermesh like a system of gears. Compared with this, man has also no absolute, but an infinitely heightened "openness to the world." The mental part of man, which makes his other unspecialization possible, is likewise unspecialized. Once again the human is elucidated by contrast with the animal. Man has, it turns out, not only rationality ahead of the animals: even within the realm of perception he has many advantages.

It was already known before Uexküll that for animals only a particular segment of the world becomes relevant, that they react only to certain stimulants and are unreceptive to others. And also before him this was attributed to the fact that the animals experience things only as they correlate with their vital interests. For the animal, the world is divided into edible and inedible, sexual rivals and sexual partners, into calming and alarming incidents. When, however, it has no vital interest in something, that thing is nonexistent for it.

But even so the animal's mode of experience has been interpreted far too anthropomorphically. It was pictured too much as if the animal were merely ignoring the thing that is of no interest to it, as man also often does. The world still seemed to be presented to the animal as it is to us, with only a graduated differentiation, first as a multifaceted objective event from which it then cuts out a narrow sector of what concerns it vitally, though a smaller sector than ours. Since Uexküll, however, we know that the animal lives primarily and only in such a sector. The only part of the world it knows is its own sector. Compared with man's, its contact with the world is unimaginably poor. It not only ignores whatever lies beyond its sector of the world but it even has no receptivity for it. Its sense organs are to some extent "filters" that allow only what is vitally significant to pass. But they are impermeable for whatever the animal does not need to know. Thus the selective function is performed already at the sensory level where an environmental sector is segmented from the total world. This segmentation is not a conscious act but takes place naturally prior to awareness. The species allows the individual animal perceptivity only for what it must perceive. The spotlight of perception, as it were, falls only on what is necessary. Thus the animal is always confined within its own world—quantitatively and qualitatively narrowed down to fit the particular species, since each has different needs and habits. It is fitted so perfectly into its world that it is not even aware of having only a segment of reality.

Uexküll's famous example is the female tick that has only three senses: sensitivity to light, odor, and temperature. With its sense of light it finds its way up a branch, and the sense of smell and temperature tell it when a warm-blooded animal passes under the branch so that it can fall on it and drink its blood. It has no eyes, ears, and taste, for it does not need them. "The entire rich world surrounding the tick thus shrinks together and is transformed into a pitiful structure consisting mainly of three qualities and three stimuli: its sector of the world." Another example: the lizard that shrinks together in the leaves at the softest sound does not react to a pistol shot near it. For a note of danger that would be connected with such a sound does not occur in its sector of the world. Therefore this sound lies beyond its threshold of receptivity.

The animal's world makes not only a quantitative selection from the world of things; it also selects only a few qualitative aspects. The animal does not have any objective "things," such as we do, with intrinsically inherent life-neutral qualities. Rather, it relates everything from the first with its own subjectivity, it asks, as it were, only: What does this mean for me as a codetermining factor of my own behavior? Therefore it is aware of only a part, and aware even of this part only in abridgement relative to itself. The world it perceives corresponds to the world it must act in.

Therefore one and the same object within the various worlds has equally various valences. For the fox that builds its den under the oak, the oak is the roof; for the owl that dwells in a high place the oak is a protective wall; for the squirrel, it is something to climb; for the birds, something you can build a nest on; the ant, however, perceives only the bark in whose hollows it seeks prey. "Every individual world cuts a certain segment out of the oak. . . . In all the various individual worlds of its inhabitants the oak plays a most changeable role, now with some, now with other parts. Sometimes the same parts are big, sometimes small. Sometimes the wood is hard, sometimes soft. Sometimes it serves as protection, sometimes for attack."

Since the Greeks the tendency has been to understand knowledge as an autonomous primal energy isolated from life and with its meaning self-contained as an absolute value. Its task seemed to be exclusively the discovery of truth. Only secondarily, it was assumed, do a few truths also happen to have a practical application. But Aristotle already knew that knowledge for its own sake is a late cultural product. And in the nineteenth century it was shown with complete clarity how much all knowledge originally aims only at the vitally relevant. If this is true for man only with limitations, it is indubitable for the animals. Their apparatus of knowledge is from the first so organized that it registers only what stands in some vital connection with them. Nature acts economically: it gives the animals no excessive organs. It is exactly the same as regards organs of knowledge: each creature has on the whole only as much knowledge as it needs to live. Knowledge beyond that would only disturb and confuse it.

The animal, however, not only perceives "less" of the world than man, but even this lesser amount has a different function for it, and that is precisely why it may be so little. The animal, as we have already said, is dominated by set instincts for each species. It does not itself decide how it will behave in each particular case: its mode of behavior is already predetermined by nature. This instinctiveness in the animal also has its effects on the world of perception and explains why things are, and need be, given to it only in fragments. Since, for each situation in which life places it, a hereditary instinct as to how it is to act lies ready in it, the animal has absolutely no need of closer intellective preoccupation with the objective constitution of this situation. It has no need whatever to penetrate the situation from all points of view. Rather, it has only to take the situation into itself sufficiently to set in motion the suitable instinctive reactions foreseen for the respective situation. But that happens on the basis of a few criteria. And so the animal can get by with a minimum of external knowledge of the world. It gets by with this minimum because knowledge of the world has a totally different function for it than for man. The impressions from the world are for it only "signals" that release a preestablished behavior mechanism. The meaning of its perception is not to communicate "world" to it, but only to communicate such signals and "effectors."

As Konrad Lorenz has shown, the animal, in addition to the action schemata of the instincts, also has receptor schemata of the world. In these hereditary codes the animal has, as it were, its "categories." It spreads them out like nets to catch the material of the world. Everything it encounters is checked by it not so much for its objective content as for whether it fits one of these schemata. If it does, the corresponding instinctive course of action is "released." The animal knows of the world only what it already knows *a priori*. It can—as Plato falsely taught of man—recognize outside only the same factors relevant to its behavior as it already bears as a general inner form within itself. Contact with reality merely provides these forms with content.[5]

Man, however, has no instincts—let this exaggeration be allowed for the sake of clarity. Nature does not say how he is to behave in a given situation. With the help of his own reflection he must determine his behavior independently, he must decide on his own how he will use the world and get along in it. He does not merely react to it, he acts upon it. But to do this he must know the world. He must have deeply penetrating and objective experience of it, as comprehensive as possible, in order to shape his behavior according to the measure of this experience. Therefore his knowledge has a completely different and broader mission in the total economy of his life than the animals' knowledge has for them. It must not only discover signals and release mechanisms but also establish a much richer relationship to reality; it must not only select a sector of the world but also bring the world to as adequate a realization as possible. What Schopenhauer said of the genius could be said of man in general compared with the animal: namely, that for man, intellect which otherwise sees the world only voluntaristically, i.e., only seeks motives for the will or the appetites in it, is emancipated from the will and open to the actual constitution of the world.

It would therefore be to stop with externals merely to say that man knows more than the animal. He does not represent a mere rectilinear progression beyond the animal. He is not merely an animal gifted with knowledge. That he knows more is based on the fact that his knowledge from the start aims for a qualitatively different purpose. And that in turn is based on the fact that his deeds and his action or inaction come about in a different manner, and on the fact that knowledge constitutes a much more relevant preparatory and intermediary factor in this. The structure of cognition here turns out to be independent of the more elementary structure of mobility. The different law of knowledge in man and animal is always correlative to the different basic law of life of the two, from which it follows, or of which, rather, it is itself a part.

Even quantitatively man's range of knowledge is much broader than what is directly important for his life. For he has first to seek out from among the neutral data those which are relevant to him, or he has to make them relevant. He must therefore first acquire a broad inventory of knowledge which will be of use to him only later—or never. His senses too are in a certain way "filters": they too, unknown to him, make a selection from the extensively and intensively inexhaustible universe. But they are much more permeable filters than the senses of the animals. Man contemplates even what is most inconsequential to him. He invents names for stars that he will never set foot on. And even the individual thing, since it is for him not merely an indicator signaling the direction he must take, reveals itself to him not only in its outlines, but with a fullness of inner treasures; not as it were only one-dimensionally, but multidimensionally from many aspects, with numerous characteristics. Of course, relatively few men take a purely intellectual interest in matters having no connection with life. Philosophy and science, which do not limit their interest merely to questions that present themselves for solution, but systematically press forward into the unknown, are late products of culture. Yet they merely extend and perfect a primary ability innate in man from the first. The animal knows naturally what it can and must know. For man, how-

ever, knowledge attains an "ethical" dimension. It becomes
for him a mission that he must fulfill but in the face of which
he can also fail.

The animal draws everything into its own vital stream, which
flows integrally from it to the world and back and thus loads
the world, too, with vital significance. In man this stream is
interrupted again and again. Between external perception
and the inner drive to action there exists a "hiatus" in him,
to use one of Gehlen's terms. To produce this hiatus he does
not need, as Scheler believed, asceticism; rather, it is inborn
and natural. What man perceives stands opposite him at a
sober distance, more remotely and strangely than for the
animal. From a mere vital correlative it becomes for man an
object with laws of its own, resting in itself and separate from
him. Or: the previous object becomes a subject, gains an
existence of its own. It no longer stands merely on the horizon
of man's vital behavior, it is no longer restricted to its narrowly defined function in terms of man in the way that the oak
is for the bird only a place for a nest, and for the ant only
something to climb on. This univocally clear context of particular utility does not exist in man. He first has not a vital
but a cognitive relationship with the oak. Therefore he comprehends it not only from the outside as the bearer of a function, but, function-free, in itself, as something with its own
individuation and center of gravity. Afterward man too makes
use of things and gives them functional value. But he does
this only after they had originally been purposeless objects.
Heidegger is wrong when he gives logical priority to the
"object as implement" (das Zuhandene) which reveals itself
to man's preoccupied determination, and considers the "neutral object" (das Vorhandene) that is "gawked at" as only a
deficient modality. This pragmatic naturalism is not confirmed
by general anthropology. It corroborates, rather, the older
classical concept that sees man as a born theoretician. Even
practical man (homo faber) is not an animal. He himself
makes his relevant implements (Zuhandenes) from the pri-

mary neutral objects (*Vorhandenes*). That is why he can recurrently change the type of implements he makes from the same objects.

Wolfgang Köhler's experiments on the intelligence of the chimpanzees are a good illustration of the differing world relationship of man and animal. Even these most intelligent animals experience no function-neutral "things," which therefore can fulfill different functions, now these, now those; they experience each thing in terms of only one function that it has for them and therefore arrive only with difficulty at the insight that one can also attach other functions to it, that one and the same thing can have several functions. Köhler's apes discovered only in a rare "*aha* experience" that a fruit attached high in the cage can, for lack of a stick (which had been taken away), also be knocked down with a blanket; this was a rare experience because the blanket serves a different purpose; it is "something to sleep on" and not "something to fetch down with."

As the animal cannot separate the thing as a whole from the role it plays in its life, it cannot separate the parts of a thing from the role which they play as a whole. It experiences a greater whole not as a composite of independent parts but from the first as a form (*Gestalt*). All partial components get their valence radiated from the form and are completely fused with one another. If therefore an animal meets such a partial component outside its form, it does not recognize it as already known in the total *Gestalt*. If a fly is thrown to a spider, it does not know what to do with it and does not suck it out, for it knows flies only within the net in which it is used to catching them. For this reason also it was not at all evident to Köhler's apes that one can replace the missing stick by breaking off the branch of a tree, for the branch has a valency in the perceptive image of the tree and is therefore something so fundamentally different from an isolated stick that the identification is not easily made. Here too, then, the object is comprehended not in itself, as an objective substance, but in the framework of a coordinate system in which it has a certain significance, and that prevents or at least hampers both its recognition outside this system and the recognition of its suitability for other significances. Thus the tendency to see forms stands in the way of real objectivity. The perception of shapes, whose presence the *Gestalt* theory also proved to exist in man independently of the functions of analytic reason, is completely dominant in the animal. Man, by analytically breaking things down into their elements, comes to experience the objective content of these elements.

With the understanding of the world, self-understanding too is transformed. The animal, which relates everything to itself and sees everything only in its own perspective, a perspective that determines value or nonvalue, takes itself as center. Man, however, lives "excentrically" (Plessner). He not only orients the world on himself but he also reorients himself by the world, localizes himself in it and knows of his accidental, arbitrary position in it. "To stand within his perspective and outside it is the position of man." Together with the world he himself becomes reflexively objectified. Here is the source of all potentiality for higher forms of introspection, self-examination, and self-education.

Uexküll himself did not yet contrast the world of the animal with the world of man. As the same thing has different meanings in the various worlds of the animals, so it is also in the worlds of different human groups. For the forester the oak is a certain quantity of wood, for the child who sees the forest as populated with hobgoblins, a frightful face stares out of the bark. For the hunter the forest is a game area, for the wanderer shade, beauty, and enchantment, for the fugitive a place to hide. According to Erich Rothacker, even entire cultures are receptively selective by characteristic dimensions and each articulates a different landscape out of the total world. The entire mental life of a Greek educated in philosophy and art is constructed differently from that of a Roman trained for dominion, law, and purposefulness. The antisensual

Anglo-Saxon Puritan remains unreceptive to certain stimuli
for which precisely the Latin strives to increase and cultivate
his sensibility. Just as psychologically there is a "threshold of
consciousness" that can be passed only by certain stimuli,
so also there is a "cultural threshold": only what has "mean-
ingfulness" within my "style of life" finds admittance into it.

But the animal has primarily and only the subjective world
given to it by nature. Man, however, has the objective world,
which he narrows down only secondarily into a subjective
one that he himself constructs. The world around man (*Um-
welt*) is part of culture. Therefore "man" in general does
not have one single subjective world, as each species of animal
as a whole does, but individual groups of men—nations, pro-
fessions, etc.—each have a different one. Very often a member
of such a group grows up into such a world; but at some
earlier time it was "created," and indeed a member of posterity
can—if he wants to or must—dissolve, change, or expand it.
The Roman can educate himself into a Greek. Man is never
restricted rigidly to one particular type of world. Therefore
man can also participate empathetically in the world of other
beings, even the nonhuman. He can even understand his
enemy.

As was already remarked above, action based on reflection
goes farther in the long run than instinctive reaction, but at
first it makes life harder; this also applies to the field of knowledge, according to Gehlen. Within a more limited circle the
animal knows from the first what each thing means and requires of him. Man, however, in his much more complex
world, does not at first know what he is to make of it and
how to move about in it. At first he enters a surprising arena
of ever new and uncoordinated impressions that stream at
him from all sides and disorient him.

Man frees himself from a flood of stimuli by letting it flow
into a network of canals consisting of cultural structures he
has built, according to Gehlen, who again is thinking in terms
of dependency where in reality mutual interconditioning is

the case. Since he has no natural points of reference by which to categorize the world, man posits artificial ones himself; only with their help does he succeed in processing the abundance of impressions, which would paralyze him by their strangeness and leave him confused; and thus he makes things "manageable." Indeed the main achievement in this regard is done by language, which in contrast with the cry of the animal expresses not merely a subjective emotional reaction but something objective, as only man can know, remember, and describe it. Language, by classifying everything under concepts, clears up the overcrowded chaos. Things gain a place in the plan of order. Without their necessarily playing a role in the events of man's life, man, by giving them a name, takes possession of them. The words of language, one could say, take the place in man of Lorenz's hereditary receptacle in the animals, except that words are not coupled with reactions, and except that they provide much more complex and differentiated receptacles.

In general anticipation, Herder, in his treatise *Über den Ursprung der Sprache* ("On the Origin of Language"), states that every animal has its own "sphere" in which it belongs from birth and in which it finds its way by its own instincts. "With man the whole scene changes." Compared with the animals he first seems to be "the most orphaned child of nature. Naked and exposed, weak and puny, timid and defenseless; and the worst of his misery is that he is deprived of any instinctive guide to life. Born with such a distracted, weakened sensuality, with so indefinite latent abilities, with so divided and sluggish drives." "The nature of his species" consists practically of "gaps and defects." But though comparison of man with the animals results to his disadvantage from many points of view, still he seems privileged and called to higher things from other points of view. "Man has no uniform and narrow sphere where only one task awaits him; he is surrounded by a world of activities and objectives." Precisely because he must penetrate a much broader circle of reality, his nature is in many ways the opposite of the animal's, which would only hamper him. "His senses and organization are not sharpened for only one thing; he has senses for everything, and therefore naturally they are weaker and duller for each particular thing. His energies of soul span the entire world; there is no direction of his ideas toward only one thing; therefore he has no innate artistic drive and no innate artistic perfection." Herder summarizes the "substitute arising from the midst of his defects" with which nature compensates him under the comprehensive term "reflectiveness." Kant adopted this idea in his *Idee einer allgemeinen Geschichte in weltbürgerlicher Absicht* ("Idea for a Universal History with Cosmopolitan Intent"). Thus Herder already sees the connection between the animal's instinctive guidance system and its confinement in its *milieu* on the one hand and man's feeble instincts and greater openness to the world on the other. And likewise Herder in his treatise recognized the special significance of language. He calls man the "creature with speech." This definition is too narrow; for man is the "cultural creature" in general; and yet Herder saw correctly for this particular segment of culture. Humboldt too showed the paradoxical simultaneity of man's and culture's development by the example of language: only by catching the world in the net of knowledge does he develop his own productivity and inner fullness of form; but in order to be able to form language, he first had to be a man.

Part 5

MAN AS AN
INTELLECTUAL BEING
(Cultural Anthropology)

CHAPTER 12

Man as the Creator of Culture

Incompletion and Self-perfection
(Freedom, Creativity, Individuality)

Cultural anthropology will be the anthropology of the future. All previous anthropology was but a prelude to it. It is the first anthropology that does not artificially isolate man from the natural world he lives in, but sees him in interrelation with it, both as its bearer and as borne by it. But the world he lives in is his culture. Thus cultural anthropology is the first to encompass the whole man.

Human "unspecialization" with respect to acquiring knowledge means, as we have seen, rephrased in positive terms, "openness to the world."

But man is also unspecialized on the active side, with respect to his behavior. He is not driven by any instinctive impulse to apply particular abilities or to observe particular living habits. Unspecialization here turns out to be indeterminacy. But this means in positive terms: first, he can determine his modes of behavior himself, i.e., he is creative; and secondly, he can be so only because he is free. He is free in the double sense of "freedom from," namely, from governance by the instincts; and "freedom to," namely, to productive self-determination. Creativity and freedom therefore are two additional *anthrōpina* in addition to mere theoretical openness to the world (which, as seen above, in turn depends on the structure of human action). Both terms do sound worn out—"creativity," mainly through aesthetic use, and "freedom," through ethical and political use. But as used in the present context in a general anthropological sense, they regain a new color. Unspecialization and specialization do not stand parallel to one another. Man does not live simply from the former as the animal does from the latter. Rather, unspecialization includes an incompletion. The world as we find it has a gap in it. Man's free creativity as he personally reflects on and invents his behavior serves to fill this gap and as it were to catch up with what specialization already gives the animal. On the human side then, only unspecialization and creativity together make up for the animals' specialization. The animal, it could be said, is by nature more complete than man. It comes forth finished out of nature's hands and only needs to actualize what is already present in it. Man's unspecialization, however, is an incompleteness. Nature, as it were, put him unfinished into the world; it did not make the final determination about him, but left him to some extent indeterminate.

Therefore man must complete himself on his own, must determine himself into something specific, must seek to solve the problem that he is to himself by his own efforts. He not only may, he must be creative. Creativity is not at all limited to a few activities of a few people; it is rooted as a necessity in the existential structure of man as such. As was said above, *homo sapiens* (man the thinker) is just as much and more *homo inveniens* (man the inventor). Uncompleted, open, inwardly infinite, incomprehensible, at the same time active and in process of becoming, man combines in himself all the traits with which the Baroque (and also the Romantic) period has been characterized since Wölfflin.

Man's self-perfection, however, does not necessarily mean perfection in an emphatic sense. It only means that he completes himself and gives himself definitive form. It can be a high or a low, a rich or a poor form. Precisely because man's essence depends on his own decision, he is by nature an endangered being. The animal, since it is not responsible for itself, cannot, it is true, rise above the form nature chose for it, but it also cannot fall below it. Man, however, has a much greater scope. As antiquity had seen: the possibility of knowledge and virtue includes that of error and vice. Man can elevate himself into an adorable marvel, but "the best in its corruption is the worst" (Aristotle): he can also use his ability for self-formation "to become more beastly than any beast" and—as Nietzsche described the ape in the eyes of man—"a laughter or a painful shame" for the one at a higher level.

A further corollary follows from the principle of self-perfection. That the animals find their nature already existent means that every specimen of a species resembles the other— and the lower the species, the more complete the resemblance. Their life is merely the playing of the behavior melody that is precomposed in the species; the possibilities of the species are merely unfolded. The individual man, on the other hand, struggling for his complete being cannot limit himself merely to being a representative of his species. The animal coincides completely with his species, man only partially so. In part he must also go beyond it, he must produce something new of his own. By virtue of his essential mission he is therefore in each case a special individual. Existentialism therefore has some truth on its side when it opposes the anthropology of "man in general": only the concrete, time-limited man is a complete man.

As a rule, of course, each individual's behavior is expected to conform with the respective traditions; this conformity, however, is not naturally but culturally conditioned. The Greeks first set the individual free and gave him permission and courage to be true to himself. Through the renewal and deepening of this beginning in the Renaissance and the Storm and Stress movement and, on the other hand, through Christianity, the independent and creative personality obligated only to itself and drawing on its own resources has become

the ethic and pathos of our world. But we do not thereby
educate just any special ability, but one that accords with the
central human destiny. We are merely going a bit farther on
the way it has always been our primeval destiny to go, by
which we became and are men.

Historical Views

That man again and again stands like "Hercules at the
crossroads" (Prodicus), that he must "choose" the paradigms
of his life (Plato), and give preference to the better (Aristotle), is an old philosophical tradition. But antiquity developed the idea only for the more narrow area of ethics, not
from the perspective of general anthropology or cultural philosophy. And thus in the classical tradition what we are to
choose between and for is always pregiven as an ideal norm.
We do have the freedom to decide, but not the more radical
creative freedom also to invent the content of what we want
to do. Only the Western modern age knows this creative freedom.

Therefore man, at the beginning of the modern era, faced
all things with a new self-awareness and laid claim to an
exceptional position. In the eternal order where God assigned
a fixed rank to everything, man alone has mobility and assigns himself his own rank. As the most admirable creature—
Pico della Mirandola writes in his *Oration on the Dignity of
Man*, following an Arabic original—man is envied not only
by the animals but even by the astral spirits, between which
two levels of being he holds the medial position and for which
he comprises a "unifying link" (already in Posidonius). For
he alone has self-determination in an otherwise fixed and predetermined world. But of course this grace also contains a
temptation.

After God created Adam, Mirandola writes, he said to him:
"We have given you no special form, no special heritage, so

that you might have and possess whatever you might wish as
accouterment. We have subjected all other creatures to definite laws. You alone are completely unrestricted, and can
pick and choose to be whatever you decide by your own
will. To your own honor, you yourself are to be your own
master and builder. You can degenerate into an animal or
lift yourself to the highest spheres of the Godhead." As for
man: "He can be what he desires. The animals have from
birth whatever they will ever have. The spirits were from
the primal beginning what they will remain for all eternity.
Only in man did the Father sow the seed of all activity and
the germs of every way of life. Who should not admire this
capacity for transformation, which resembles the chameleon's
and Proteus'?"

A further factor connected with this—also in Ficino and
Giordano Bruno—as the mirror image of a world which is
now experienced as infinite, man too is now to have not only
a single possibility; he ought to realize an infinite number of
possibilities. He has no definite form in which he ought to
stand still and remain after he has attained it: from every
achieved form he must develop further to the next. He is
eternally in search of himself. Involved by nature in incessant
movement, man always has an element of dissatisfaction in
him. "Only man never rests in this present state of life, only
he is not contented in this place." As for Nicholas of Cusa,
our knowledge, a living image of the world, is never perfectly rounded out and only translates objective infinity into
infinite time, so we too are in life incessantly becoming and
dying. Thus the Renaissance charged man with that restless-
ness and dynamism, with that intense desire for the new,
which, though man in fact again and again found new forms,
the Renaissance first intensified into a conscious ethic and
which since Spengler has often been called "Faustian" after
Goethe's symbol:

> In progression he found torment and joy,
> He, every moment unsatisfied!

For Herder the animal is only a bowed slave; man, however, is "creation's first freedman," "organized for freedom"; "no longer an infallible machine in nature's hands, he himself becomes the purpose and goal of his own action." That is the cause of his greatness, but also a risk. "Let us reflect how much nature, as it were, ventured, since it entrusted reason and freedom to so weak an earthly organism. . . . The scale of good and evil, of false and true, depends on him: he is to choose." Perfectibility and corruptibility are equally contained in him, and no one but he decides whether the road will lead upward or downward.

Kant and Schiller, however, fall back on the weaker concept of antiquity. Thus Schiller says in his *Über Anmut und Würde* ("On Charm and Dignity"): "In plant and animal, nature not only points out the objective, it also carries it out by itself. But to man it merely assigns the objective and leaves its fulfillment to him." Thus "nature" still establishes man's pattern. He only has to realize it. He has the freedom to decide whether he wants to fulfill it or not; only he wills, while the other creatures, both animals and God, between which he is again placed in Schiller's *Eleusisches Fest* ("Eleusinian Feast") must be what they are. But still this is only a limited freedom. It does not apply to the contentual concept of what he ought to be. (In addition, it is true, Schiller did discover the other, deeper formula of freedom, that man reconciles the realm of necessity and the realm of freedom in an aesthetic "game," "and he is fully human only when at play"; this is the point of departure for Huizinga's *Homo Ludens*.)

For Kierkegaard also each individual is responsible for himself. We cannot accept ourselves as given, we must consciously take over and "choose" ourselves. But the great "either-or" between which the Kierkegaardian choice takes place already exists as such before us. It is only the old religious choice: either Christ or Adam, either eternal salvation or earthly welfare. Kierkegaard too thus knows only the freedom of decision between preexistent values, not, however, the freedom of forming the values oneself.

It is quite a different matter with the other two great thinkers of the nineteenth century, Marx and Nietzsche. For social reality and the class situation—in Marx's too-often-quoted sentence—determine consciousness only partially. This is true with respect to secondary, i.e., philosophical or ideological awareness. But a more primary awareness, the agent intellect, has always in turn determined social reality. Marx is thus not so much an opponent of Hegel as he himself believed. He too, rather, is an heir to German Idealism, which he is merely the first to apply to the social and economic sphere and to which he gives a more radical turn. According to the classical economic theory, man has natural needs that the economy finds already existent and can only satisfy in a better or worse fashion. For Marx, however, man is even in his material needs not a natural being. He differs from the animals already by the fact that he creates his external living conditions himself, invents tools, produces wares. Indeed, in changing his living conditions he also changes himself. Man is the only creature that must work; but his work is not only a burdensome necessity, it also contains the seeds of his greatness. Just as the work of art produces a public capable of enjoying beauty, so economic production creates consumption, namely the specific need itself. Production "produces not only an object for the subject, but also a subject for the object." By satisfying the need, it first evokes it. What seemed to be our nature is really—despite all differences one is reminded of Fichte—the result of our own spontaneous activity. And as man shapes himself as an economic subject and gives himself a "finish," so also in noneconomic matters. Marx even wants to trace man's upright gait back to an achievement of the will.

Comparably, Nietzsche's primary experience of man is that of his unlimited plasticity. Completely adaptable, man can assume the most varied forms; he gives them to himself. "In

man creature and creator are united." As Michelangelo saw
beforehand the statue he had to chisel out in the marble
block, so for Nietzsche there are dormant in man—not as
original dispositions but as free designs—ideal images of
himself. "Ah, you men, I see an image sleeping in the stone,
the image of my images! Alas that it must sleep in the hardest,
ugliest stone!" (*Zarathustra* II. 2.) Man's fantasy and unrest
will forever be setting up such new ideal images for him to
guide himself by. No mode of existence to which he has
specified himself is definitive, each must "for the sake of the
future" be broken again. Man is "more insecure, more changing, more indeterminate than any other animal. . . . He has
dared more, innovated more, spited and challenged destiny
more than all other animals together: he is the great experi-
menter with himself, unsatisfied, unsatiated, struggling for
ultimate dominion with animal, nature, and gods; he is the
still undaunted one, the eternally future one, who finds no
rest from his own pulsing energy, so that his future cuts re-
lentlessly like a spur into the flesh of every present." (*Genealogy of Morals* III. 13.) His greatest danger would be "that pre-
mature stopping which, as far as we can see, most of the other
species of animals have reached long ago."

A part of these ideas finds its modern expression in existentialist philosophy. Bergson already had warned against understanding our own psychology by the criteria of objects in the
world among which we live and which therefore are the
primary determinants of the category system of our mind. For
those things are unchangeably circumscribed. They can be
measured and counted. But the deepest wellspring of our soul
is a contourless streaming, open to the future. We must, as
Jaspers demands, deobjectify our self-understanding. Only
then can we recognize ourselves as open, unprejudiced possibility. We must decide freely about our respective being.

Therefore Heidegger has us "design" ourselves. We always
project our designs beyond ourselves; then afterward we fill in

the designs with reality. As the care of existence in general forces us to run ahead into the future of things, we do the same with our own future. Only too easily do we, in so doing, fall into the danger of not hearing the voice of our own particularity and seizing only opportunities that come from outside, imposed by impersonal social forces. Existentialist philosophy seeks to stir us up out of our dull, irresponsible dormancy in subjection to impersonal forces that relieve us of the decisions we must make. It wants to be an appeal to us to draw on inner potentials that are appropriate to our own self and only to it.

The freedom to design ourselves, however, is limited by certain pregiven facts. First, human existence never begins from anew, rather it always finds itself "cast" into a historical situation, which it has not sought. We are all shaped by the traditions of communities in which we grew up and are. We are shaped by our own past. This "heritage," whose bearers we are, also prescribes the lines for our future. The possibilities we decide for are only then most deeply our own, if they are in continuity with this heritage. Thus the sovereignty over one's decisions at any moment is limited by the weight of past life.

As existence does not begin from nothing, it does not hang in empty space. It not only stands in a general historical situation, but it faces the tasks of a concrete situation of life. These tasks too are among the premises of our decisions. We can solve the tasks in this way or that; but that we have to solve them at all, or just these particular tasks—this framework of our decisions does not lie within our power to decide.

Like Kierkegaard, Heidegger expects us to break through to our "particularity." More clearly than Kierkegaard he knows that the content of our particularity will be different for each individual. But, again like Kierkegaard, he leaves this content already pregiven at each stage. Our achievement ought to be only to be true to it, to "realize" the determinately avail-

able "possibility." He is unaware of the still more basic
achievement that consists in creating the content oneself.
But this is precisely the achievement that Jean-Paul Sartre
requires of us. Plant and animal need merely fulfill the law
of their species. Even an object of craftsmanship is produced
according to a plan located first in the mind of the craftsman.
For man, however, all Platonism fails. For man, as for no
other creature, no essence precedes his existence. Neither did
God make him in his image, nor does reason contain a pattern reflecting a timeless essence of man. Even to speak of a
human nature is deceptive; there is only a *"condition hu-
maine."*

Instead of having the permanent nature typical of other
beings, man is in the situation of always creating himself.
Since he is based on no plan, he designs himself. "Man invents
man." In an incessant surpassing of himself, he never exists
statically: he is cast again and again into a virginal future,
becoming what he wants to be.

Therefore man is condemned to freedom; he stands under
the necessity of always having to be free. Freedom is not a
gift that he can accept or reject. It is a corollary of his inner
indeterminacy as the positive pole to a negative one. "The
coward makes himself cowardly; the hero makes himself
heroic. The coward always has the possibility of no longer
being cowardly, and the hero no longer heroic." Man is inescapably free, even when he does not know it or denies it.

One could also say: man is damned to freedom. It is the
basis of his "dignity," but at the same time it charges him
with the burden of responsibility. Again and again he therefore seeks to rid himself of the responsibility that is imposed
on him: he appeals, for instance, to God's decree, which does
not exist, or to temperamental dispositions and external cir-
cumstances, which, however, all have the strength of conditioning factors and not of determinants. What he makes of
his destiny, how he shapes it, what it means interiorly for him,

depends only on him. We can never unload our responsibility. We are what we have made of ourselves.

Sartre's Promethean creationism runs into error by its very exaggeration. First, just as Valéry preferred to write his poems in full awareness rather than under inspiration, so for Sartre too man ought to "make" himself aware. But the Storm and Stress movement already knew that we do not have the capacity to make a work of art but that it must ripen in the subconscious silence of organic growth. Likewise we too must leave ourselves to our growth. It is no accident that for Sartre anthropology narrows back down to ethics: decisions that are made consciously tend to be ethical in nature. Secondly, all creation obtains its nobility only by carrying out objective necessities. Therefore for Plato it is subject to an idea, for Kant to a universal legislation. Of course these formulations have paled somewhat today when we are more aware than earlier times of the unrepeatable singularity of each individual. But even the most independent individual must be legitimated by a law, an "individual law" (Georg Simmel). If this law is missing, then creation degenerates into play. Its results no longer bear the stamp of necessity, but of whimful arbitrariness. Such a process of degeneration did take place in the transition from the Storm and Stress movement, in which the creative subject had a feeling of unity with nature, to Romanticism, which let the subject be held and borne by nothing higher. And this subject, condemned actually no longer to freedom but to whimfulness, is also Sartre's subject. As a philosopher he is therefore unwittingly the heir of Romantic disorientation and unrestraint. Thirdly, because in our creativity we are dedicated to something that goes beyond us, we may not ascribe what we create only to ourselves. Other forces are at play in its origin. This is true when we create structures and when we create ourselves. We receive ourselves "as a gift" (Jaspers). Fourthly, that the thing created never is a mere deposit of our conscious creative intent, which we directed at it, is also evident because it contains aspects which were not included in the original intention and of which there is no trace in reality. "I brought pure fire from the altar; what I lit is not pure flame" (Goethe). We are surprised at the results of our own action.

The Solidified Self-perfection of Culture

But one does not arrive at the decisive distinction between animal and man as long as the comparison is made only on the animal and physical level: the animal has these qualities, man those. Man has more ahead of the animal than mere qualities. What keeps him alive and makes his life easier is something else.

Man does not have to start all over again at every moment to gain insight into and knowledge of the things of the world and to decide on his own behavior. Every individual collects "experiences" and such "experiences" are also handed down in every group. A store of knowledge thus always stands at man's disposal. The same is true of technical inventions, which compensate for man's lack of adaptation to nature, and also of moral and social institutions that survive: they do not disappear soon after they are discovered but they become a permanent property that accompanies the nations. Along with the ability to create them we also have the ability to preserve them as a firm institution and traditional value. Actual creativity of the present is, as it were, joined by a second aggregate condition of creativity: the creativity of the past which has crystallized into objective form.

We call the solidified sediment of human creativity "objective spirit," thus broadening the extension of a Hegelian term. If we add to this the stock of knowledge that is acquired but not created by man, then we speak of (objective) culture. Although culture comes only from man and in order to remain alive needs him as its bearer to use it and fill himself with it, still it is not merely an accident of man, but it has independent existence outside him. This is evident from the fact that it can be separated and transmitted from one bearer to the other. To this extent it stands separate from us just as does the pregiven world of nature. We stand just as routinely and inescapably within the cultural world we ourselves produced as we do in nature.

Therefore it was one-sided to endow man with free decision only on a logical and ethical plane. Anthropologically it is just as important that the decision need not be exhausted in life but that on the basis and as a result of it a particular structure of reality can be consolidated. What at first was lived or produced by only a single individual can become the norm imitated and followed by the feeling and action of posterity. *Homo creator* is immortalized in his cultural creation. The triumph of his creativity is cultural creation.

Cultural creation has a much broader scope and goes much deeper than was formerly believed. In human life much less is based on natural disposition than on culturally shaped form and usage. As we learned historically that there is no natural man, but that even the earliest man lives in a culture, so we have learned anthropologically that even the most elementary and necessary things—how we feed and procreate, in what relation we stand to the world around us, how we are to bring up our offspring, etc.—even all this, which we actually share with the animals, but which in them is regulated by nature, is left to man for his own management. We ought not to appeal to a prescription of nature for any solution which we choose. Neither for marriage nor for communal life, etc., can it be proven from nature that just this and no other form is the right one. All our regulations are, if you will, unnatural and artificial. They are based, to use the terminology of the Sophists, not on nature (*physis*) but on custom or convention (*nomos*)—which could have originated, however, as some Sophists maintained, from a purely arbitrary decision, though in subjective good faith that they were necessary and right of themselves. Nature itself forces us to have culture. It is our nature that even on the animal level we freely acquire the forms our life will take by cultural creativity. Even this level is in man a cultural level. Again this shows that man is not an animal with the specifically human traits merely added to this animal foundation; the human is all-pervasive and starts from the ground up.

However, we must feed ourselves, we must have relations with the other sex. What we determine ourselves is only the forms in which we want to do this. The necessity is anchored in nature, only the manner is left to us. There is a condominium of necessity and freedom. Once man has been endowed with culture-creative energy, he applies it beyond the necessary and creates cultural forms not at all foreseen by nature, and for which not only the manner but even the fact stem from his own free actions. Doubly creative, he not only gives a naturally necessary area its form but he even creates the area itself.

When Franklin called man "a tool-making animal" he was expressing only the least part of the truth.[1] Man makes not only tools but traditions of knowledge, world views, technologies, mores, social orders, means of communication, styles, and many other things.

Generally we take all this for granted and do not imagine that one could think or act otherwise. Although man is in fact the originator of his culture, for the longest time he was not aware of this. He considered it a gift of God or a natural endowment. The creativity objectively at work had not yet been discovered subjectively. Then the Greeks, who stood under the pressure of a multiplicity of cultures and for whom the otherwise infinitely slow pace of cultural development had accelerated so much that culture became visibly recognizable as man-made, established theories of the origin of culture. The modern age and the men of today are even more deeply aware that everything cultural—whether it is the same or different elsewhere—had a historical origin; they are aware how wide the circle of man-made things extends.

CHAPTER 13

Man as a Creature of Culture

The Cultural Being

We have studied man as a creature of God, as a rational being, and as a living being. Now we must get to know him as a cultural being. First we are the producers of culture. But then by a retroactive effect we are also produced by it. In a "mighty system of circular causality" (Kroeber) we determine it and then in turn experience its "patterning" of us. Theodor Litt, dealing with the problem of the "individual and society," is right when he speaks of a "reciprocity of perspectives." Looked at from the point of view of culture, active productivity is primary. It is the foundation of culture. Viewed from the perspective of the individual, however, the fact that one is a passive product is primary. Each person is first shaped by culture and only then does he perhaps also become a shaper of culture. Not only the possibility of individual cultural achievement but also the tide of inherited objective culture fills the "gap" that man seems to have, compared with the animal. That mankind always lives in a double historical awareness, that it sees itself as at the same time young and old, and as standing at the beginning and at the end, is rooted in this. Both are true: as still creative into the future it is young; as already created by the past it is old.

As was said above, no one ever starts "right from the beginning." Not every situation challenges our creative originality. Generally we need only adopt the results of earlier creativity. We can sail on an extensive canal system that was excavated by others long before our time. We are born not only with our own gifts as individuals but simultaneously into the "external apparatus" of a culture that has been accumulated by our ancestors and handed down to us. In addition to our subjective spirit that we bring with us we receive from them the gift of objective spirit. Our life need only, as it were, be poured into the tracks of this objective spirit which are available to us. For long stretches it needs absolutely no spontaneity, but merely reactualizes preexistent patterns of life. As with ethical norms, we are led by the hand by preexistent norms in all fields.

That is the only way for us to maintain ourselves in a strange and hostile world and at the same time reach a much higher stage than we could attain by ourselves. What the individual can invent in his short lifetime is relatively little. In culture, however, our basis is the collected wealth of experiences and inventions that an entire people, indeed all nations, have undergone during many generations. We are beneficiaries of this wealth and our work is made easier and more differentiated by this preparatory work which others have done.

The psychosomatic constitution that man gets from birth is still not everything. It is only a part of his total reality. As long as one asks only about man's psychosomatic qualities, one will fail to understand him. Man can be completely understood only by studying his roots in objective spirit in addition to these qualities, and cultural conditioning in addition to the natural qualities he gets from birth; by studying, in other words, not only the eternal and constant heritage of his species but also that which, though likewise inevitably belonging to the species, varies in content from people to people, from age to age. Each human individual becomes such only as a participant in the supraindividual medium of culture, which surpasses the individual and is common to an entire group.

Only its support holds the individual upright; only in its enveloping atmosphere can he breathe. Its directives interweave in him like a system of blood vessels that constitutes an integral part of him. This system must, it is true, be filled with the blood of his subjectivity; he must, so to speak, fill the ideal with the reality of life. Culture would not exist without man to fulfill it. But he would also be nothing without culture. Each has an inseparable function for the other. Any attempt to separate these two intermeshing parts from this unity must necessarily be artificial.

The Social Being

That the individual as he is born and considered only of himself is still missing something was always implicitly known in all social anthropology, which thus stands on a higher level and makes a more modern impression than psychological anthropology. For the psychic sphere (although culturally modifiable) is part of the natural structure of man. It remains relatively identical from culture to culture. The social, however, though required as such by nature, constitutes a part of culture as far as its particular form is concerned. In every culture it is differently constituted. Thus if man is seen as a social being, he is also seen as a cultural being.

Aristotle knew that man needs this cultural complementation, that he is not sufficient to himself but is by nature a social being. Whoever stands outside the community is not a man but "either an animal or God." This took Aristotle beyond his usual rational anthropology—for reason belongs to us as individuals. "Man becomes a man only among men. If men are to exist at all, there must be several" (Fichte).

The community, however, is not only itself a cultural sphere; it is at the same time preserver and transmitter of the total culture. In order therefore to be cultural beings in the full sense, we must first and foremost be social beings. Therefore

man is the most social being and this does not contradict the
fact that he is at the same time the most individual being.
He is social as a creation of culture; he is individual as its
creator.

Many animals also live in groups. But, for man life in the
group has an additional, deeper function. An animal that
grows up separated from other members of its species—for
example, among men—will still behave exactly like one that
grows up normally. The specific behavior develops in the
animal by itself. But man becomes a complete man only by
growing up in a tradition-bearing group of his own kind. His
cultural side can develop only in that way. If he grows up
in isolation, he remains mentally at the level of a child. And
if he grows up among wolves (the werewolf) or bears, the
impulse to imitate his surroundings is so strong that he assumes the habits of these animals. Linnaeus even cites such
wolfmen and bearmen, who have been found from time to
time, as a separate variety of men (*homo ferus*), and he
stresses that they lack upright gait and speech.

Therefore it still is insufficient to understand man only from
his social context. Generally the right idea is also meant when
this is done, but the emphasis is falsely placed. That we belong to a social structure does not of itself alone constitute the
completion of humanity in us. This happens only through participation in the goods of culture (including the nonsocial
ones). True, the social structures transmit culture to us. The
road to participation in culture passes via participation in the
social. But the social is only a precondition of the cultural.
From an anthropological point of view, we have to be socia-
ble only in order to attain what is more decisive, namely, to
become cultured. Therefore social anthropology falls short of
the mark. Only cultural anthropology reaches the center of
the problem.

The Historical Being

But one could just as well speak of historical anthropology as of cultural anthropology. This states outright a point that was only implicit until now. For, precisely speaking, man does not produce culture, he produces cultures. That man, as was seen, may on the basis of his indeterminacy give himself his own form, must be supplemented by the statement that in the course of history (and in different parts of the earth) he has repeatedly given himself different forms, indeed an infinite variety of different forms. Just as the self-formation that the individual acquires necessarily always has an individual stamp, so also does the comprehensive cultural self-formation of nations and epochs. Man's cultural nature therefore includes historicity. This was already known at the beginning of the modern era: for thousands of years the bee has been building the same cells, but man "progresses." As a cultural being he is a historical being too. And this also in a double sense: he both has power over and is dependent on history, he determines history and is determined by it.

This fact is overlooked whenever it is assumed that there is such a thing as a natural culture (a "natural state," a "natural religion," etc.) contained in man's nature as a timeless *a priori*, whether one naïvely equates one's own views and habits with this natural culture or looks upon it as an ideal that was realized in the past or will be realized in the future. If that were so, then all our cultural production would face only the task of discovering that aprioristic image of an intrinsically necessary and solely appropriate natural culture and translating it into reality. And we would be truly creative only negatively, i.e., when we failed to attain it.

Such a natural culture remains a dream and an illusion. Every appearance of naturalness is deceptive. The cultural could be defined radically as the historically variable. What is innate in man and could be called our *a priori* is not a pre-existent norm of culture, but a functional energy: only the undifferentiated capacity to design culture and to work toward it. But in content we remain unbound. Our creativity is not limited by a primeval goal that need merely be recognized; it is total creativity. Even the setting of the goal is within our competence. It can produce cultures most varied in content. The scope of this is unforeseeable; it is not limited by a finite number of possible contents. Our creativity is inexhaustible. Certainly the variety of cultures is based on the particular temperament of races and individuals, and on geographical and other conditions; yet the cultures are ultimately never merely the development of an inner factor or reaction to an external one, but they are a free creation. This is what constitutes our power over history.

In order to salvage faith in one culture predicated by God or nature, despite the empirical multiplicity of cultures, the historical events have been forcibly interpreted as a process involving unilinear progress toward it or decline from it or both—in which case it is shifted to the central position. This process is conceivable as a single development embracing all mankind or as repeated in each nation. In either case, the multiplicity of cultures is seen in a purely negative light. It is just as opposed to the one ideal culture as the multiplicity of errors is to the one truth.

Nothing is changed by distinguishing more precisely between various stages of the process, such as the old theory (revised by Morgan and refuted by Eduard Hahn) that every people passes through the stages of gatherers and hunters, shepherds and farmers; or Wundt's theory that each goes through the three religious stages of animism, fetishism, and totemism, or a minutely differentiated series of phases that takes place within total culture, as depicted by Lamprecht and Spengler. This apparently pluralistic philosophy of history in fact worsens the mistake. It not only has the ideal form of culture be anchored as the ultimate goal in human nature but also the defective forms, and not only their content but also their number and sequence. Not even the culturally negative still remains within the power of our creative freedom. Both the true and the false lie preformed by nature in us, like later teeth in the child's jaws. The nations are to a certain extent put on one track, from which they cannot deviate, and on which they must race again and again past the same stations—if possible according to a prescribed schedule. They already contain all cultural possibilities as fixed dispositions and must merely rattle them off in a stereotyped rhythm of development like a well-memorized lesson.

Contrary to this, the historical thinkers of the Goethe period, Herder, and the Romantics recognized that different cultures and different modes of development of particular cultural fields can be equally valid. Not as if everything that ever saw the light were ipso facto equivalent. Intrinsic standards of value are retained as before. But it is in principle inadmissible to measure, for instance, earlier or other art by the stylistic norms of one's own or by an artistic ideal, as had formerly been done. Everything that has grown organically and with genuine necessity contains an ultimate meaning and stands at the same level. This conviction reached by the philosophy of history made the old traditional schematic curves of history obsolete and also imparted on historical research, with its loving contemplation of foreign cultures, the intensity it has had since then.

The insight of the Goethe period into the legitimate plurality of cultures was, however, still lacking an anthropological foundation. That foundation is provided only by the modern image of man as primevally incomplete and therefore necessarily seeking completion in new cultural creations. The Goethe period was, indeed, as no prior era had been, aware of the creative. But it limited this to the artistic genius. Only modern thought has expanded it into a fundamental anthropological and cultural-philosophical principle. The absolute, which man always hoped in vain to find in the objectivization of culture or of a particular culture, resides in fact in his subjective creative power, which produces all cultures, and this counterbalances the mutual relativization of cultures. The philosophy of history, already in the Goethe period, and anthropology, which has reached maturity in the present, are like two sides of the same coin and verify each other.

As was stated above in general, we are not only builders of but also built by culture; the individual can never be understood by himself alone, but only from the cultural preconditions that support and permeate him. This is also true concretely. As we can never produce culture in general, but rather a historically particular culture, so the retroactive influence of that culture always makes historically particular men of us. Our freedom to create history is counterbalanced by our being bound within it, by productivity on the one hand, by plasticity on the other, and so man is changed along with his changing milieu. We not only imitate what has previously been lived in the culture that surrounds us—"as the old sang, so the young twitter"—but even the things we produce are impregnated with its overall style. We are far more strongly determined by cultural factors than by hereditary factors—which race theoreticians consider the only decisive ones. Citing some examples from Rothacker: Bach's identical twin in a strange cultural circle would not have become Bach; a European born with artistic talent, if he grew up in Japan, would paint in a Japanese style. Our different pasts make us different. Each culture, after man has formed it, forms man in turn, so that indirectly he forms himself by forming it. Therefore today cultures are frequently depicted from an anthropological point of view in books with titles such as *Hellenic Man, Gothic Man, Protestant Man,* etc.

Just as there is no eternal ideal pattern of culture, there is no such pattern of man. By assuming a different form in every culture, man is not deviating from a form he should have. As variability is the law of culture, so it is the law of man. In fact, it is a law of culture only because it is one of

man. Man does not have an intrinsic being that remains im-
mutably the same, while history unrolls only in the outer
regions. Even for spontaneous actions apparently independent of history, such as loving and praying, we have no guide-
lines valid once and for all as to how we should perform
them: down to our deepest interior we are committed to a
fate of historical mutability. The fundamental equivocity of
man is always clarified by the historical place where he is.
What history makes of him is no less himself than what nature
makes of him. "I am history as much as nature" (Dilthey).
Indeed, "man has no nature, he has only a history" (Ortega
y Gasset). But the two things are not contradictory: as Democritus formulated it, education, by transforming man, creates
another nature (*physiopoiei*).

But if he is so subject to mutability, what does man's constant nature consist of? How can we define him? Or does the
unity of being a man break apart? "The type 'man' melts in
the process of history," says Dilthey. And he concludes,
"What man is, he discovers not by pondering over himself,
but only through history." Since man exists and gains definite
contours only as historically specified, then apparently our
only recourse is to stick to the testimony of history, which
spreads before us the infinite inventory of his specifications.
We know no more about him than it teaches. A general philosophical anthropology, on the other hand, whose statements
apply to man in general and which therefore would be ante-
cedent to the historical sciences of man seems to be illusory.
Just as since Romanticism historical disciplines have replaced
systematic ones in the objective study of culture (as, for example, the history of literature replaced poetics), so the systematic analysis of man himself seems to have to yield to historical study. What was philosophy has become history. As a
generation later in existentialist philosophy the individual rebelled, so in Dilthey history rebels against man in the abstract (to this extent the two are related).

But despite the confusing divergence of his historical modes of appearance, there must be something immutable in man's nature that holds them all together. All the historical faces that he gives himself are indeed transitory and exchangeable. Whoever proclaims one of them to be the only suitable one for man, as was formerly done, can be correctly reminded of their multiplicity and equivalence. But what turns out to be a human trait remaining perennially amid all change is that man may and must again and again give himself his features from his ultimate amorphousness, this intermixture of unstructuredness, plasticity, and the mission of self-education. What he gives up when he no longer thinks of himself from within a certain culture he regains as another power that makes all cultures possible (according to Plessner). Man as made by man (*homo hominatus*), as a concrete phenomenon, is historical, but his creative core as self-creator (*homo hominans*) is eternal. In this sense a human "nature" does exist: but it cannot be thought of in terms of content but only in terms of a law of his constitution prior to all contents, not as a result but as a process that produces the results and is intended to do away with man's primordial incompleteness. True, that the process leads to any result at all, like a geometrical locus of the possible results, also is an inextricable characteristic of man. But the completions change, while the incompletion and the process of completion itself remain identical. The phenotype of man, one could say, always surpasses his genotype in content. We can always give only a temporary clarification for the "open question" (Plessner) that we always remain for ourself at the heart of our being.

The Traditional Being

The instincts that control the behavior of animals are a natural property of his species. They are transmitted in the same way as physical traits, purely biologically by heredity. Therefore, as was seen above, an animal brought up among creatures of another species behaves just as if it had been brought up by its own parents. Human behavior, however, is controlled by the culture which men have once acquired. How man feeds and procreates, how he dresses and dwells, how he behaves practically and ethically, how he speaks and looks at the world, all the cultural forms he makes use of, are based on historical creation. Since they have been historically created they cannot be transmitted by heredity. Yet they must be preserved: what the ancestors have discovered must benefit later generations. Instead of heredity then, another, purely spiritual form of preservation must be used. This other form of preservation is called tradition. Through it, knowledge and skills are passed from generation to generation like buckets in a fire line and transmitted to posterity by example and instruction from their predecessors.

In historical (or, at first, mythological) memory we are aware of the distance in time that separates us from the past, and we perhaps even know the exact length of this distance. The past is something unique that never returns. Tradition, however, knows no distance; rather, the past extends relevantly into the present. It is forever repeated anew by it. Therefore we generally do not know where traditions come from. The earlier the stage a people is at, the more the past lives for it only in the form of tradition. What is to be kept is built into the tradition; when it finds no place in real life, then tradition finds one, for instance by the establishment of a yearly recurring feast day, on which the event is reenacted.

The individual first has to absorb the cultural traditions that reach him. He must first climb to the height of the culture he was born into. Let us take language as an example. What man receives as an innate disposition of nature is only the ability to speak as such. But the historical and individual language spoken in his surroundings, is not innate in him. For it is a creation of history. He must instead acquire it receptively from the outside. If he grew up in other surroundings, he would speak another language. And if he had no one at all to teach him a language, he would, despite his inborn ability to speak, remain dumb. The fact that, on the one hand, man may produce culture corresponds to the fact that, on the other hand, each one who comes later must learn this cultural material.

As learning is one half of tradition, teaching is the other. Much, of course, need not be consciously taught. Children reproduce it by themselves because of their natural readiness to imitate, and because they can count on the recognition of their elders only by doing so. But other things have to be inculcated into them expressly, and often with much toil; they have to be educated into the tradition by a long-lasting process (while animal parents only rear their brood, which can rely on genetic dispositions, and train them to a much lesser extent). After man has produced culture he must, through education, see to it that it is not lost again; and this is not merely aiding a natural process that would develop anyway. This is the anthropological basis of all education.

If we examine man, as it were, macroscopically, studying peoples and eras in the multiplicity of their styles, then we can define him as the creative being that always produces new cultures out of himself. But if we change lenses and contemplate the individual within these cultures, then, to our surprise, what characterizes man on a broad scale does not occur in the individual, or does so only partially. For the individual, and not only the average one but even the greatest genius, is much less the former of culture than one who is formed by it. Compared with the immense predetermination which he owes to his culture, his ability to determine anything is very limited. As he bases himself on previous creations and uses them, what he creates himself seems to be slight and only a most internal secret cell or emergency reserve of his being, by which one cannot however understand him as a whole. Although freed by nature, not only to fill out preexisting schemata of being or behavior but also to act originally, man too is made a filler of such schemata by the tradition he grows up in: though not defined by nature, he is defined by cultural schemata invented by his ancestors, who thus limit the principle of originality in their progeny. Between his original disposition to individual decision and his simultaneous necessity to rely on a tradition, in which decisions are preempted and co-opted and which he must merely imitate, there is an antinomical clash. The human trait of being completed by a culture neutralizes that of autonomous self-completion and lets it shine through only dimly.

But the contradiction is only apparent. Both human traits can and must coexist. Fortunately everyone is embedded in a tradition. Thanks to it, one can call more numerous and higher cultural goods his own than he could ever gain by himself. Nonetheless the obtaining of new knowledge is not taken away from him; it is in fact expected. For first of all the traditional patterns have gaps. They do not regulate life down to every detail. Again and again man comes to a situation where the patterns are missing and he is alone and must discover his way by his own judgment. Furthermore, they are not absolutely clear: they need interpretation, or at least allow for interpretations. Finally they are not rigid. Here too tradition differs from heredity, whose much more absolutely binding course allows for no deviations (or only for such as are followed by the whole species). After all, we always retain a certain distance from tradition, from which we either affirm or deny it. Where it no longer corresponds to our feelings, we can abandon it or rebel against it.

The new knowledge we have gained, the invention we have made, the mode of behavior we have brought to the light for the first time can either disappear again immediately or remain limited to one individual. Or they can enter into the tradition, can transform it and so introduce a change for others too. Although tradition is the principle of conservation, it is alterable, and, because created once itself, it is accessible to enrichment and modification by new creation. It did not arise earlier all at once either. It sums up a multiplicity of individual

achievements. And this process of accretion still continues today and into the unforeseeable future, so much so that finally,
as Simmel has shown, the individual can no longer assimilate
everything that objective culture offers him and can no longer
acculturate himself subjectively by doing so. And as successively new elements are added to it and likewise transmitted
by it, other elements undergo a transformation, while yet
others die out. Man's body, in which the law of heredity
prevails, is relatively unchanged from that of his remotest
ancestors, but each subsequent generation finds itself spiritually in a different world.

Not every change of tradition, of course, results from a
conscious intention. Languages, mores, styles, etc., often develop by immanent laws without anyone intending it, in fact,
as Simmel has shown, even contrary to man's will: these
changes follow the particular logic of their products. Even
where such a will is prevalent and at work, its bearers need
not be aware of it, and therefore they need not stand out as
individuals. The real subject of the development can be an
anonymous collectivity. As it can take place unwilled or not
consciously willed, so also can it go unnoticed. Each individual
and generation may subjectively believe that they are merely
passing down their age-old traditions faithfully to their offspring. But in fact they change them. When two generations
do the same thing, it is no longer the same, and in the course
of long periods of time something new in principle arises
through an accumulation of slight modifications. But the
change becomes visible only where earlier documents have
been preserved.

This impersonal form of change is predominant mainly in
early times. For the deeper we go back into history the more
piously we find men clinging to their inviolable traditions.
The traditions were considered sacred as ancestral heritage
and community property, and they were preserved from
generation to generation down to the present. Every deviation
from them could call forth the anger of higher powers, could

cast the community into misfortune. Therefore every violation was punished as sacrilege. So at this stage, only such changes could take place as either did not cross the threshold of consciousness or could appeal to a higher sanction and necessity. Only late, only in higher cultures and after repeated loosening from the Greeks on, did tradition gradually lose its rigidity. The "constraint" (Durkheim) which it exercised on the individual decreased. He has gained greater leeway against it and can disregard it to develop his own creativity. In great individuals, whose works everyone admires and who invent new directions for the life of later-comers to follow, mankind thus honors, as it were, crystallization points of its own creative power. They are the representatives of humanity (Emerson).

Purely from logic one might think that in the beginning the least was created and therefore the creative gift could develop most unrestrictedly; conversely, one might think: the more there has already been created, the less the field of application creativity finds, and so it must recede. In reality it is most restricted at the start by traditionalistic coercion, and finds insufficient groundwork and possibilities of combination. Of course an excess of already created materials can cause it to recede again. Thus the creativity of the individual can apparently advance most unrestrictedly in the middle stage of a culture. Here it has its greatest blossoming. Universal necessary tasks still exist and save productivity from declining into mere play and whimsicality. The most favorable times are the transition periods when an old world-structure is collapsing but individualism has not yet reached its peak.

NOTES

Chapter 2. Prephilosophical Anthropology

1. But later, on a higher level of reflection, Schiller and Goethe again approved the anthropomorphism of the gods because of the intensifying effect which it has retroactively upon man. "Since the gods were still more human, men became more divine" (Schiller). "The meaning and intent of the Greeks is to divinify man, not to humanize God. What they practiced is theomorphism, not anthropomorphism." (Goethe.) Indeed, Goethe's pantheistic world view does not allow for a qualitative break between man and God:

> The question still remains,
> Whether they were gods or men?
> Thus Apollo was in the form of a shepherd
> And the most handsome of them looked like him;
> For where nature rules in its pure cycles
> All worlds interlock.

2. In most languages the word for man, in the sense of "human being," is of relatively late origin, but already in the Indo-European it was derived from the word for man (the male of the species). In primitive times the male was considered the human being *par excellence* (therefore the name for woman was derived from his). Franz Bopp traced the word "man" back to the root found in the Latin *mens* ("mind") and *memini* ("to remember"); but even if he is right, the equation, man = the thinker, would be etymologically risky. Whether in the puzzling word *anthrōpos*, the first half is cognate with *anēr* ("the male") is doubtful. The Latin *homo* is

etymologically cognate with *humus* ("earth," "ground"), but this does not signify, as Schrader believed, that he sprang from the sacred marriage of heaven and earth, but that he was "earth-bound" in contrast with the heavenly gods; cf. the Greek *brotos* ("mortal," "earthly"). Similarly, the Hebrew *adam* comes from *adama* ("earth")—though perhaps it does not mean "the earthly one" in general, but "the one made from the earth" of the Genesis narrative.

3. Based on Jüthner, *Hellenen und Barbaren* (1923).

4. This more intellectual conception, however, never did gain general acceptance. Because of his mother's nationality, Demosthenes' opponents, for instance, called him a barbarian Scythian who merely used the Greek tongue.

5. Cf. Richard Reitzenstein, *Humanität im Altertum* (1907), and M. Schneidewin, *Die antike Humanität* (1897), pp. 31 ff.

6. Zeno, the founder of the Stoic school of philosophy, had developed a remarkable plan for combining all men on earth into one world state, and Plutarch recognized that this idea did not stem merely from Stoic philosophy, which considered all men to be equally rational creatures, but that Alexander's military campaigns contributed to it, because he did in fact establish a world empire. Christianity too speaks of a universal "greatest city" (Augustine) and a worldwide monarchy (Dante).

7. Zosimus, though he is admittedly a late witness (a historian of the fifth century A.D.), reports the belief that "the whole human race," including the barbarians, though it was not permitted for them to be initiated, was held together by the mysteries of Eleusis.

8. According to Hans Plischke, *Von den Barbaren zu den Primitiven* (1926), and Raoul Allier, *Le Non-civilisé et nous* (1927).

9. Cf. Hölderlin's letter on the Germans: "You see craftsmen, but no men, thinkers but no men, priests but no men, masters and servants, but no men."

Chapter 3. Selected Data Toward a History of Anthropology

1. Cf. F. Heinimann, *Nomos und Physis*.

2. Even the purely optical seeing of oneself in a mirror has, as poets have often described it, a touch of weirdness about it that we usually shy away from. In a Chinese myth, each man has a

more genuine self following him, but the moment he looks back and catches sight of himself, he dies.

3. Heidegger, *Being and Time,* pp. 71 ff.

Chapter 4. Anthropological Content of the Old and New Testaments

1. Therefore Christ calls himself "the Son of Man," i.e., the second Adam. Similarly in the Rig-Veda, "Manus" is the proper name of the first man and also the designation for all the "children of man."

2. Eckermann (October 7, 1828) reports a conversation of Goethe's with a natural scientist who tried to substantiate the legend of Holy Scripture with the argument that nature acted very economically in all its productivity. "I have to contradict this opinion," Goethe said. "I hold, on the contrary, that nature always acts copiously, in fact wastefully, and that it is in better accord with its usual pattern to assume that instead of beginning with a single scanty couple, she originally produced men by the dozen, indeed by the hundreds. The learned men who wrote the Word of God were concerned primarily with their Chosen People, and so I would not at all contest the origin of this people from Adam. But we others certainly had other progenitors."

3. Karl Barth gives a collection of interpretations in his *Church Dogmatics* III. 1. 194 ff.

4. It is a widespread religious conviction that there are taboos against knowledge as well as other areas of taboo.

5. It has once again become a hypothesis of modern anthropology that the origin of man had to take place in a paradisiacal environment and that from there man first gained strength for a harsher mode of life. For man, in his instinctual poverty, can nourish and protect himself from the cold and other animals, etc., only with the help of cultural inventions. But how was he supposed to survive in the interim between his origin and the first inventions? Obviously only under relatively safe and copious, i.e., paradisiacal conditions.

6. Cf. also Shakespeare (*Hamlet* II. 2): "The beauty of the world! the paragon of animals! And yet, to me, what is this quin-

tessence of dust?" Similarly Rückert: "Let the idea that we are only men keep you from arrogance; but that we are indeed men give you confidence and joy."

7. According to Hans von Prott (whom Stefan George praised as "having seen the Olympian gods for a second"): "*Mētēr*, Bruchstücke zur griechischen Religionsgeschichte," *Archiv für Religions-Wissenschaft* 9, 1906.

8. The saying "What does it profit a man, if he gain the whole world, but suffer the loss of his soul" also means only: ". . . if he still must die."

Chapter 5. Five Main Theses of Religious Anthropology and Their Rebuttal

1. Nietzsche's aphorism (in *The Will to Power*, "Critique of Religion") sounds like a paraphrase of Feuerbach: "All the beauty and loftiness which we have conveyed on real and imaginary things, I wish to reclaim as the property and product of man: as his most beautiful justification. Man as poet, thinker, God, love, power: alas for his regal generosity with which he has endowed things only to impoverish himself and feel miserable! His greatest selfishness till now has been that he admired and worshiped and managed to hide from himself that he had created what he admired." George's stanza is in the same tradition:

> Where once they became, they must go light
> The wicks for upper gliorioles.
> They go down each earthly day
> And bow in service to an earthly sole.

2. Cf. the anthropological outline in Xenophon, *Memorabilia* I. 4, and IV. 3, and also Cicero, *On the Nature of the Gods*, §§ 133–167.

Chapter 6. The Glorification of Reason

1. The concept of the microcosm was devised by the Greeks (Democritus; cf. W. Jaeger, *Nemesios von Emesa*, 134 ff.) and

later revived by Renaissance philosophy (Campanella), and by Lotze and Scheler. But it always was a stumbling block to Greco-Roman and Western thought. For we (like the Bible) tend to look upon man as something unique, recurring nowhere else in the cosmos.

Chapter 7. The Dethronement of Reason

1. Since the "exceedingly gifted Greeks" magnified the mind, it is only logical for Klages to reach back before the Greeks for his model of the past. In search of a pre-Homeric, philosophical and cultic stage of religion, Friedrich Schlegel had discovered a passage in Herodotus (*Euterpe* 52) which attributed such a religion to the Pelasgians, the mythical aborigines of Greece. The "Pelasgians" passed from Schlegel to Creuzer, from Creuzer to Bachofen, from Bachofen, with whom Klages became acquainted through Karl Wolfskehl, to Klages himself, who therefore is connected by a direct line with Romanticism. The role of the Pelasgians for Klages is filled by Gondwanaland for a related thinker, Edgar Dacqué. Even externally—this theory claims—men who lived on this vanished continent were not the same as modern *homo sapiens*. Man, in this theory, had an organ which we have lost, an eye on his forehead (as the cyclops legend recalls) through which he had better perception of nature than we do and saw directly into the mysteries of the universe.

Chapter 9. Man's Place in the Animal Kingdom

1. A zoological atlas still popular today avoids the embarrassment of placing the races of man immediately next to the animals by depicting them on the very first page, ahead of the title and introduction, thus keeping a distance between man and the animals even in the external layout of the book.

Chapter 10. The Theory of Evolution and Its Opponents

1. Similarly Hegel does not scruple to rank Christ within the total course of world history: for he considers world history as a whole to be salvational history. Shortly thereafter, however, Strauss considers this same concept of Christ to imply a "de-divinization" and profanation. In both cases the transition from the Goethe period to the nineteenth century perverts an identical thesis into its opposite.

2. Karl Wolfskehl's expression "the origin of man—a primeval event before the beginning of time" derives from Darwinism but sublimates it into poetic lore.

3. Under Haeckel's influence, the German industrialist Krupp offered a prize for the answer to the question: What can be learned from the theory of evolution for domestic policy?

4. But Fabricius (1748–1808), a student of Linnaeus, had assumed that "sooner or later new creatures will evolve from man, with greater perfection, greater knowledge, greater powers, just as man himself has evolved from the animals."

5. In this context it should be noted that the so-called "missing link," the connecting species between ape and man, whose supposed nonexistence was exploited by Darwinism's opponents, was discovered in 1936—the *australopithecus transvaalensis* (whereas the falsely so called *pithecanthropus erectus*, or Java and Peking man, whose fossil remains had been discovered earlier, was in reality the oldest, though still primitive, type of man). Since *australopithecus* (also called *plesianthropus* or *paranthropus*) was not a tree-dwelling arm swinger, but lived on a bushy plateau, the much-talked-of "descent from the trees" may never have taken place or at least not immediately as the first step in man's origin.

Chapter 11. The Human Structure

1. Since domesticated animals also become instinctually impoverished, the conclusion seems plausible that man too is a result of domestication—self-domestication, so to speak (Lorenz). In a domesticated animal the instincts recede, because it becomes accus-

tomed to being taken care of by another being (i.e., man). It does not develop other abilities to compensate for the missing instincts. Man, however, from the start, has no instincts, for he disposes over completely different abilities, for which reason he needs no instincts. Accordingly, a "wild form" of man, more gifted with instincts, never did nor could exist.

2. Only man, said the eighteenth-century thinker La Mettrie, could die of starvation in the middle of a river of milk. "Nature had created us to stand below the animals in order to glorify all the more the miracle of education which alone lifts us above this niveau and ultimately places us above the animals."

3. According to the anthropobiologists Broom and Washburn, man's vertically erect stance had the unintended side effect of enlarging the brain and increasing intellectual abilities, which man thus attained only by a fortunate accident. First came two-footedness; then the humanization of face and brain (made possible by the freeing of the hands and the use of tools) followed as a second step in the origin of man. The body was human before the mind was.

4. The two lines of thought were already contrasted in Greco-Roman antiquity. Anaxagoras claimed that man was the most intelligent animal because he had hands. He thus did not deduce the plus from a minus, but the mental plus from a physical plus. Aristotle, however, held the opposite: because man is the cleverest of creatures, he also has hands.

5. But man too is, though to a lesser extent, ruled by such patterns of receptivity. That is why we consider the eagle proud, the camel arrogant, the cliff a threat, the quarter moon a girl. According to C. G. Jung, our experience is categorized in archetypal patterns. This also applies to the individual: in each person, habits of apperception develop and solidify. "Finally one experiences only oneself" (Nietzsche). Therefore time goes faster with age: one no longer experiences anything new.

Chapter 12. Man as the Creator of Culture

1. But animals also have tools as such. Isn't the spider's web a tool? But the spider spins its web only by a natural capacity, and

it must spin the same web again and again. One can put a board down next to a stream a monkey wants to cross, he will not use it as a bridge. He lacks the imagination to discover the inner form "bridge." Man, on the contrary, develops his tools, inventing different ones for different purposes.

SELECTED
BIBLIOGRAPHY

This abridged bibliography lists translations instead of the original German works, whenever available. However, it was impossible to eliminate German titles completely. Comprehensive classified bibliographies of the entire field of philosophical anthropology are available in Michael Landmann, *Philosophische Anthropologie,* 3d ed. (Berlin: de Gruyter, 1969), pp. 201–213, and, by the same author, *De Homine* (Munich, 1962), pp. 543–614.

Alsberg, Paul, *In Quest of Man: A Biological Approach to the Problem of Man's Place in Nature.* Pergamon Press, 1970.

Althaus, Paul, *Paulus und Luther über den Menschen.* Gütersloh: C. Bertelsmann, 1951.

Bally, Gustav, *Vom Ursprung und von der Grenze der Freiheit. Eine Deutung des Spiels bei Tier und Mensch.* Basel: B. Schwabe, 1945.

Barth, Karl, *Christ and Adam: Man and Humanity in Romans 5,* tr. by T. A. Smail. Harper & Brothers, 1957.

Benedict, Ruth, *Patterns of Culture.* Houghton Mifflin Company, 1934.

Binswanger, Ludwig, *Being-in-the-World: Selected Papers,* tr. by Jacob Needleman. Basic Books, Inc., Publishers, 1963.

Boas, Franz, *The Mind of Primitive Man.* The Macmillan Company, 1911.

―――― *Race, Language and Culture.* The Macmillan Company, 1966.

Boer, Wolfgang de, *Das Problem des Menschen und die Kultur. Neue Wege der Anthropologie.* Bonn, 1958.

Bollnow, Otto Friedrich, *Das neue Bild des Menschen und die pädagogische Aufgabe.* Frankfurt, 1934.

—— "Existenzerhellung und philosophische Anthropologie," *Blätter für deutsche Philosophie,* Vol. XII, 1938.

Brüning, Walther, *Philosophische Anthropologie.* Stuttgart: E. Klett, 1960.

Buber, Martin, *Between Man and Man,* tr. by Ronald Gregor Smith. The Macmillan Company, 1965.

—— *The Knowledge of Man: Selected Essays.* Harper & Row, Publishers, Inc., 1965.

Buytendijk, F. J. J., *Wesen und Sinn des Spiels. Das Spiel des Menschen und der Tiere als Erscheinungsformen der Lebenstriebe.* Berlin, 1933.

—— *Woman: A Contemporary View,* tr. by Denis J. Barrett. The Newman Press, 1968.

Carrel, Alexis, *Man, the Unknown.* Harper & Brothers, 1935.

Cassirer, Ernst, *An Essay on Man: An Introduction to a Philosophy of Human Culture.* Yale University Press, 1944.

Coon, Carleton Stevens, and Hunt, E. E., *Anthropology A to Z: Based on the Work of Gerhard Heberer* (tr. by Hans Gunthart *et al.*). Grosset & Dunlap, Inc., 1963.

Davis, Kingsley, *Human Society.* The Macmillan Company, 1949.

Dinkler, Erich, *Die Anthropologie Augustins.* Stuttgart, 1934.

Dobbek, Wilhelm, *J. G. Herders Humanitätsidee als Ausdruck seines Weltbildes und seiner Persönlichkeit.* Braunschweig: Westermann, 1949.

Eichrodt, Walther, *Man in the Old Testament.* London: SCM Press, Ltd., 1966.

Gehlen, Arnold, *Der Mensch. Seine Natur und seine Stellung in der Welt.* Frankfurt: Athenäum, 1966.

Groethuysen, Bernhard, *Philosophische Anthropologie.* Munich, 1928–1931.

Guardini, Romano, *The World and the Person,* tr. by Stella Lange. Henry Regnery Company, 1965.

Gutbrod, Walter, *Die paulinische Anthropologie.* Stuttgart: Kohlhammer, 1934.

Häberlin, Paul, *Der Mensch. Eine philosophische Anthropologie.* Zurich, 1941.

Hartmann, Nicolai, "Naturphilosophie und Anthropologie," *Blätter für deutsche Philosophie,* Vol. XVIII, 1944.
———— *New Ways of Ontology,* tr. by Reinhard C. Kuhn. Henry Regnery Company, 1953.
Heidegger, Martin, *Being and Time,* tr. by John Macquarrie and Edward Robinson. Harper & Brothers, 1962.
Heinimann, Felix, *Nomos und Physis.* Basel: F. Reinhardt, 1945.
Hengstenberg, Hans Eduard, *Philosophische Anthropologie.* Stuttgart, 1966[3].
Herskovits, Melville Jean, "Anthropology in 1945," in *Britannica Book of the Year 1946.* Encyclopaedia Britannica, Inc., 1946.
———— *Man and His Works: The Science of Cultural Anthropology.* Alfred A. Knopf, Inc., 1948.
Jaspers, Karl, *Man in the Modern Age,* tr. by Eden and Cedar Paul. New and corr. ed. London: Routledge & Kegan Paul, Ltd., 1951.
Katz, David, *Animals and Men: Studies in Comparative Psychology.* Longmans, Green & Company, 1937.
Kluckhohn, Clyde, *Mirror for Man.* McGraw-Hill Book Co., Inc., 1963.
Köhler, Wolfgang, *The Mentality of the Apes.* Harcourt, Brace & Company, Inc., 1925.
Kraeling, Carl Hermann, *Anthropos and the Son of Man.* Columbia University Press, 1944.
Kroeber, Alfred Louis, *Configurations of Culture Growth.* University of California Press, 1944.
———— *The Nature of Culture.* The University of Chicago Press, 1952.
———— (ed.), *Anthropology Today.* The University of Chicago Press, 1953.
Landmann, Michael, *De homine. Der Mensch im Spiegel seines Gedankens.* Freiburg, 1962.
———— *Der Mensch als Schöpfer und Geschöpf der Kultur.* Munich, 1961.
Landsberg, Paul Ludwig, *Einführung in die philosophische Anthropologie.* Frankfurt: Klostermann, 1960.
Leeuw, Gerardus van der, *Religion in Essence and Manifestation,* tr. by J. E. Turner. Harper & Brothers, 1963.

244

Lepenies, Wolf, and Nolte, Helmut, *Kritik der Anthropologie*. Munich: Carl Hanser Verlag, 1971.

Linton, Ralph, *The Cultural Background of Personality*. Appleton-Century-Crofts, Inc., 1945.

Litt, Theodor, *Mensch und Welt*. Munich: E. Reinhardt, 1948.

Löwith, Karl, *Meaning in History: The Theological Implications of the Philosophy of History*. The University of Chicago Press, 1949.

Lorenz, Konrad, *Evolution and Modification of Behavior*. The University of Chicago Press, 1965.

———— *King Solomon's Ring: New Light on Animal Ways*, tr. by Marjorie Kerr Wilson. The Thomas Y. Crowell Co., 1952.

———— *Studies in Animal and Human Behaviour*, Vols. I and II, tr. by Robert Martin. Harvard University Press, 1970–1971.

Lowie, Robert Harry, *An Introduction to Cultural Anthropology*, new and enlarged ed. Farrar & Rinehart, Inc., 1940.

Malinowski, Bronislaw, *A Scientific Theory of Culture, and Other Essays*. University of North Carolina Press, 1944.

Mead, Margaret, and Métraux, Rhoda B., *The Study of Culture at a Distance*. The University of Chicago Press, 1953.

Miller, Hugh, *Progress and Decline: The Group in Evolution*. Pergamon Press, 1964.

Mouroux, J., *The Meaning of Man*, tr. by A. H. G. Dowens. Doubleday & Company, Inc., 1961.

Mühlmann, Wilhelm Emil, *Geschichte der Anthropologie*. Bonn: Athenäum, 1948.

———— *Homo creator*. Wiesbaden: Harrassowitz, 1962.

Murdock, George Peter, *Social Structure*. The Macmillan Company, 1949.

Niebuhr, Reinhold, *The Nature and Destiny of Man: A Christian Interpretation*. 2 vols. Charles Scribner's Sons, 1941–1943.

Otto, Rudolf, *The Idea of the Holy*, tr. by John W. Harvey, rev. with additions. Oxford University Press, 1936.

Pappé, H. O., "Philosophical Anthropology," in *The Encyclopedia of Philosophy*. The Macmillan Company, 1967.

Peursen, Cornelis Anthonie van, *Body, Soul, Spirit: A Survey of the Body-Mind Problem*, tr. by Hubert H. Hoskins. Oxford University Press, 1966.

Pieper, Josef, *Leisure, the Basis of Culture*, tr. by Alexander Dru.

Rev. ed. The New American Library of World Literature, Inc., 1963.

Plessner, Helmuth, *Laughing and Crying: A Study of the Limits of Human Behavior*, tr. by James S. Churchill and Marjorie Grene. Northwestern University Press, 1970.

——— *Die Stufen des Organischen und der Mensch. Einleitung in die philosophische Anthropologie*. Berlin, 1965².

Portmann, Adolf, *New Paths in Biology*, tr. by Arnold J. Pomerans. Harper & Row, Publishers, Inc., 1964.

Redfield, Robert, *Human Nature and the Study of Society*, ed. by Margaret Park Redfield, Vol. I. The University of Chicago Press, 1962.

Riezler, Kurt, *Man, Mutable and Immutable: The Fundamental Structure of Social Life*. Henry Regnery Company, 1950.

Rothacker, Erich, *Probleme der Kulturanthropologie*. Bonn: H. Bouvier, 1965².

——— *Philosophische Anthropologie*. Bonn: H. Bouvier, 1966².

Scheler, Max, *Man's Place in Nature*, tr. by Hans Meyerhoff. The Noonday Press, 1962.

Schoeps, Hans Joachim, *Was ist der Mensch? Philosophische Anthropologie als Geistesgeschichte der neueren Zeit*. Göttingen: Musterschmidt, 1960.

Schwidetzky, J., *Das Menschenbild der Biologie*. Stuttgart, 1959.

Siegmund, G., *Der Mensch in seinem Dasein. Philosophische Anthropologie*, Teil I. Freiburg: Herder, 1953.

Sombart, Werner, *A New Social Philosophy*, tr. and ed. by Karl F. Geiser. Princeton University Press, 1937.

Steinbüchel, Theodor, *Vom Menschenbild des christlichen Mittelalters*. Tübingen, 1953.

Stürmann, J., *Systematische Anthropologie*. Munich: M. Hueber, 1957.

Teilhard de Chardin, Pierre, *Man's Place in Nature*, tr. by René Hague. Harper & Brothers, 1966.

Thielicke, Helmut, *Death and Life*, tr. by Edward H. Schroeder. Fortress Press, 1970.

Thirring, H., *Homo sapiens*. Vienna: Ullstein, 1947.

Thomas, William Isaac, *Primitive Behavior: An Introduction to the Social Sciences*. McGraw-Hill Book Company, Inc., 1937.

Tillich, Paul, *Der Mensch im Christentum und im Marxismus.* Stuttgart, 1952.

Tinbergen, Nikolaas, *The Study of Instinct.* Oxford University Press, 1951.

Torrance, Thomas F., *Calvin's Doctrine of Man.* Wm. B. Eerdmans Publishing Company, 1957.

Uexküll, Jakob von, and Kriszat, G., *Streifzüge durch die Umwelten der Tieren und Menschen.* Berlin: J. Springer, 1934.

Wein, Heinrich, "Von Descartes zur heutigen Anthropologie," *Zeitschrift für philosophische Forschung,* Vol. II (1947).

―――― *Das Problem des Relativismus. Philosophie im Übergang zur Anthropologie.* Berlin, 1950.

Weizsäcker, V. von, *Der kranke Mensch. Eine Einführung in die medizinische Anthropologie.* Stuttgart, 1951.

Wiese, L. von, and Specht, K. G., *Synthetische Anthropologie.* Bonn, 1950.

Ziegler, K. (ed.), *Wesen und Wirklichkeit des Menschen, Festschrift für Helmut Plessner.* Göttingen, 1957.

Zimmerli, W., *The Law and the Prophets: A Study of the Meaning of the Old Testament,* tr. by R. E. Clements. Harper & Row, Publishers, Inc., 1967.

INDEX